# Really Sharp Piecing

by
Barbara Barber

**G Charney**
**BOOKS**

G Charney Publications
Ramridge Dene, Ramridge Park,
Weyhill, Andover, Hants SP11 0QP


ISBN 0 9530848 0 9

Design by Colin Currill Creative Services


Printed in England by KNP Group Ltd

*Title Page Illustration:*
**Goato and Friends,**
83" x 83"
by Barbara Barber, Hampshire, England
Collection of the Museum
of the American Quilter's Society,
Paducah, Kentucky, USA.
*Photo courtesy of the American Quilter's Society.*

# CONTENTS

*To my parents, Alfred and Dorothy Ploug,*
*with love.*

## ACKNOWLEDGMENTS

I thank all of my students and all of the quilters I come into contact with for their inspiration and the enrichment they add to my life.

I would like to thank Lois Andrews, Maggie Barber, Phoebe Bartleet, Cathy Michel Corbishley, Veronica Gilberts, Myra Ibbetson, Shelagh Jarvis, Shirley Shotton and Julie Standen for their enthusiastic help in making quilts for this book and also for allowing me to include photographs of some of their other work.

I also thank Shirley Bolt, Sarah Hadfield, Angela Hodge, Sally Laine, Linda Park, June Thorpe, and Sylvia Vance for allowing me to use photographs of their work.

I give a special thank you to Jan Luckhurst and June Thorpe for proofing the patterns.

I thank Peter Gibson-Barnfather for his help with the illustrations.

I thank my daughter Eliza for her understanding nature and always being willing to lend a helping hand.

To say thank you to my husband and soul-mate, Peter, would be inadequate. Not only did he do most of the numerous drawings for the book but as always, he has continually helped and strengthened every part of my life.

Peter and I give a very special thank you to Colin Currill without whom this book would never have been completed. His technical help has been invaluable and it has been a real pleasure for us to work with him.

# INTRODUCTION

Basically this book introduces the methods I have developed using foundation piecing for full circle designs. It also shows ways to use straight line foundation piecing for improved accuracy. You can get rid of your fear of curved seams for once and for all. The methods are easy but best of all they work!

In November of 1992 I designed my quilt Solstice. At that time I was still fairly new to quiltmaking as I had started quilting in May 1991. I felt that the design was a good, strong design but knew that making it successfully by traditional piecing methods was probably beyond my abilities at that time. Also, the idea of cutting out all those tiny triangles accurately definitely did not appeal to me.

Gradually the idea of foundation or paper piecing Solstice formulated in my mind. It wasn't difficult for me to see that foundation piecing would work in the blocks for both the blue and green triangles which have a "flow" of pieced triangles with a definite beginning and ending. What about those full circle stars in the sashing which were so necessary to the design? They were circular and therefore did not have a beginning or an ending. It took a while, but suddenly I thought - why not make a beginning and an ending by slicing into the circle? By leaving seam allowances, one could always re-join the circle when finished with the piecing. I'd be using the tried and true method of foundation piecing, so it would be very accurate, even in a full circle.

In 1993, I made Solstice and it was a very successful quilt for me, winning awards both in this country and in America. Whenever it was exhibited, the question I was most frequently asked was "How did you get all those tiny points so sharp?" From Solstice, there followed my workshop, video and now this book. Quilters love the workshop and the video because they offer a very easy and relatively fast method of ensuring total accuracy in their work. This is particularly helpful when piecing circular designs.

June Thorpe, quilter, teacher and especially, friend, named my workshop "Really Sharp Piecing". The name stuck - not only to the workshop and video but also to my original block that I had used in the sashing in Solstice.

As with all methods of foundation piecing, it does waste some fabric but I have taught the "Really Sharp Piecing" workshop many times and have never had a serious complaint about the fabric wastage. I think the reason for this must be that time is precious to us all and to piece this type of work using the standard methods would be very time consuming. Although I've had no complaints about fabric wastage I have had many a student come up with ingenious uses for the off-cuts. In this book, there is a pattern for a quilt made with the off-cuts from an other one.

At the beginning of my workshop, I always give a warning - "EXPECT TO BE CONFUSED". Then I give words of comfort - "DON'T WORRY - IT WILL ALL SUDDENLY BECOME CLEAR" - and it does. So as you read the book, don't be surprised if you are feeling a little confused. When you are actually doing it and have the photocopies and fabrics in front of you, things will become much clearer. In workshops, the students have successfully pieced the Really Sharp Piecing Block and you can do it, too.

If you feel hesitant to try designs which require curved seams, you're not alone! When faced with my first curved piecing in Solstice, I was terrified. In workshops, students also strongly express this fear of curved piecing. Whilst working on Solstice, I developed a method which dealt with those fears for once and for all. I don't promise you 100% perfection on your very first attempt but after just several goes you, too, will be freed from this fear of sewing curves. With that freedom comes the ability to sew a whole new range of very exciting designs with your sewing machine.

Not all of the designs in this book feature circular piecing. This is a book of techniques using foundation piecing. Yes, it works very impressively with circular designs and makes a block that looks incredibly difficult to piece, very easy to piece. So easy, in fact, that I have taught it successfully to beginners. However, this method has many more possibilities than just those that involve circles. You can apply these techniques to other shapes such as squares, octagons, hexagons, ovals or even triangles and rectangles.

It has also become the method I use to very accurately piece long, straight sections of triangles or bias squares.

It is this accuracy which makes it such a valuable technique. Blocks which would be impossible to make with traditional methods suddenly become not only possible but easy.

I do so hope you enjoy this book and utilise the techniques in it. Whether you make the quilts as presented or just use parts of them to design your own is up to you. The possibilities are endless and since designing the quilts for the book, I keep coming up with more and more ideas for this type of foundation piecing. So put on your thinking cap and let your mind wander and come up with your own new variations. They're there - just waiting for you to think of them!

*In Quiltmaking,*
*Any design is feasible, Any technique is possible*
*For*
*Necessity is the Mother of Invention*

# HINTS, TIPS and GENERAL GUIDELINES

Before starting to make any of the quilts in this book, I would strongly advise you to read through the book first. This will give you the best understanding of the whole process. As a self-taught quilter, I can say from experience that some of the very best information I have gained has been gleaned from what may at first appear to be the rather tedious introductory sections of a book.

In this chapter you will find general information which will help you to get the best results with the greatest ease. Below is a list of materials and equipment followed by miscellaneous information in which you will find hints and tips to make this type of quiltmaking easier. Some of this information is crucial to success with the patterns.

## MATERIALS AND EQUIPMENT

*Sewing Machine* - Foundation piecing really has to be done by machine but you can use any age or model sewing machine.

*Needles* - I do a lot of machine quilting and when quilting I use only the sharpest and newest of needles. After quilting for a while and feel I need to change the needle I don't discard it. I put those needles in a little bottle and save them to use in foundation piecing projects because the needle is going to dull quickly anyway as you're sewing on paper. My choice of needle is size 80 for almost all the quiltmaking I do. In foundation piecing, a size 90 needle will make slightly larger holes as it pierces the paper and should make removing the paper easier. You may like to try the larger needle if you do not have a stash of size 80 needles from machine quilting projects.

*Straight Pins* - A good quality pin is very helpful, making a quality finish easier to obtain. The best pins are the long, thin ones with flat "flower" heads. They are more expensive but last a long time and make a world of difference. It is so much easier to work accurately with these finer pins. Thicker pins tend to make the layers shift as you insert them, even if you've lined the edges up very carefully. This is especially true when pinning through paper.

*Rotary Cutting Kit* - Rotary cutting is a time saving method of cutting which has become a part of most quilters' lives although I must confess to firmly believing for about two weeks that it was the most useless thing I'd ever bought! Now, of course, I wouldn't do without it and am endlessly finding new uses for the big 15" square ruler. If you have a spare rotary cutter, you may want to use one for cutting paper and save one exclusively for cutting fabric. Although using a rotary cutter will certainly speed the process up, all of the quilts in this book could be made using scissors but you would need to draw seam allowances onto some of the patterns.

*Fabrics, Thread & Wadding* - The single most important thing to consider with these items is quality. To produce a quality quilt you must start off with top quality materials. Your work is worth it and deserves it. I love 100% cotton for my work and therefore use cotton fabrics, cotton thread and cotton wadding. The fabrics have all been pre-washed in the way in which I intend to wash the finished quilt. You don't have to use cotton, of course, and I have seen silks used very successfully in Really Sharp Piecing workshops.

For me, however, cotton has such a forgiving nature and is naturally engineered to last a lifetime or two. If all of the materials in a quilt are made of the same thing, it only stands to reason that they will 'wear' at the same pace. A polyester thread could cut through a cotton fabric over a period because it is stronger. This is an important consideration when paper piecing as the stitches are so tiny. I use 100% cotton thread.

As for wadding, my personal favorite is 'Softouch' by Fairfield. It is 100% cotton with a lovely feel and quilts beautifully by either hand or machine. There are many other excellent choices for wadding but please be sure to select a quality filling for your quilt. Choose one that won't let your work down and will last as long as your quilt without bearding or disintegrating.

*Spray Starch* - It's wonderful!! I spray starch all the fabrics I use in almost all of my quilts. There simply is no comparison between working with a "firm" or a "flimsy" fabric when doing intricate work. The "firm" will always win and the time spent starching will be more than made up for by the time you save in the ease of putting your quilt together. Aside from making the fabrics easier to work with, starch stabilises the fabrics, making bias edges much less likely to stretch.

I use spray starch but you could just as easily use dip starch. The reason I use a spray is for convenience. I only spray the estimated size piece of fabric I need when I need it. There is no way I would consider starching my whole fabric collection - but then again I know I will never use my whole collection, so I work on the basis of starch-as-you-go. Having said that I use a spray starch, I feel I should add that I also use a mask or spray outdoors when starching to protect me from inhaling the fumes.

Estimate the approximate amount you will need of a certain fabric and add a little to that for leeway. Then cut it off from the bulk of your fabric and starch just the amount you need. I usually spray three lighter coats rather than one heavy coat of starch as I've found the iron likes this method best. Be sure and iron the fabric completely dry between each coat. The starch does cause a build-up to form on the iron but this is easily removed. Let the iron cool down and then remove the starch with a damp cloth. After starching be sure to clean the iron before pressing fabrics whilst sewing. The amount of starch you use is up to you but my guide is, the more intricate the work, the stiffer I starch. There have been times when my fabrics have been very stiff indeed.

All of the quilts in this book have been made with pre-washed 100% cotton fabrics. The fabrics have all been well starched before cutting out the required pieces. All of my work is quilted by machine and I do think that the starch is an asset to quality machine quilting. However, if you are going to quilt by hand I urge you to rinse the starch out of the finished quilt top before layering it up with the backing and wadding because otherwise you will find it very hard work getting the needle through the starched fabrics, particularly where there are seams involved.

*Iron* - Do not use steam when starching or with freezer paper. I like to press each seam as I sew but if you have starched the fabrics well it isn't so vital as the starched fabrics finger press very well indeed. As for the use of steam in general, well, if you ask 20 quilters their view, you could easily end up with 20 different opinions on the pros and cons of steam. Like a lot of quilters, I have a strong personal preference - no water is ever put into my iron.

*Design or Pattern Sheets* - All of the designs in this book are sewn on paper and therefore you need adequate copies of each design to make a given quilt. Some of the designs will fit on a page and are to be found on the pages dealing with that quilt. Often the patterns are larger than a page

and you will find them on pullout sheets, labeled appropriately, folded and tucked into the pocket in the back cover. If your design is one which fits on a page, the spiral binding will make photocopying much easier. NEVER cut into or sew on these design sheets - to do so would mean that you have lost your pattern for good. Each project will tell you which patterns you need and how many photocopies you will require to complete the quilt. If you need to glue photocopies together to make a block, do this before starting the quilt.

*Freezer Paper* - Freezer paper has many varied uses in quiltmaking but mainly it is used as a means of easily making accurate and re-useable templates. One side of freezer paper is plain paper which you can mark with a pen or pencil. The other side has a thin plastic coating. A desired shape of freezer paper can be applied to the fabric, plastic side (shiny side) down and ironed on. The heat from the iron melts the plastic coating and adheres it to the fabric but later can be easily and cleanly lifted off. It can be re-used a number times before it looses it's ability to stick to the fabric. When I need a template for a large odd-shaped piece in a quilt, I use freezer paper. It is easy to use, inexpensive and very accurate. Freezer paper is available from quilt shops in Britain. In the US , it is available from both quilt shops and supermarkets. I am continually finding new uses for freezer paper which make my quilting life easier.

■ For the quilts in this book, yardage is calculated for 44"- 45" wide cotton fabrics, assuming 42" useable width. There is 5% allowed for any shrinkage that may occur when you wash the fabrics. Nothing is more frustrating than running out of a certain fabric and not being able to buy more of it to finish a quilt. Most of the quilts in this book are of the scrap type and running out of a particular fabric for this type of quilt can often lead to some very creative and pleasing results. However, this would not be the case if half-way through piecing Solstice *(page 84)* or Columns *(page 52)* you ran out of any of the fabrics. When I made Solstice, I underestimated the amount of orange fabric I would need. At that time, orange was not a popular colour and it was impossible to find a perfect match. A very slow and painstaking process of over-dying did finally achieve the match I needed but it took me a week to do it. Bad experience is the best teacher, or so they say, and I have erred on the side of caution ever since.

■ After choosing a quilt you want to make, be sure to read through the pattern completely before starting the quilt.

■ Seam allowance is so much more important than you might think, especially when doing this type of work. The seam allowances for the foundation piecing is not important just so long as it is adequate; an approximate $^1/_4$" will do nicely. Most of the quilts have foundation pieced units or blocks combined with traditionally pieced sections. Using the methods in this book, you can be assured of an accurate $^1/_4$" seam allowance when joining foundation pieced units to other pieces of the quilt because you will be stitching on a drawn line. For the best results, please check that you are also stitching a true $^1/_4$" seam when sewing seams which are not stitched on paper. Many problems can be averted by taking the time to get your seam allowance right. Best of all, once you've sorted it out properly, it will stay sorted, and will be one more problem that you can put behind you for good.

■ Each pattern will say when to remove the paper foundation. Do not remove it before reaching that stage.

■ You may find it helpful, for the first few times you do this type of piecing, to write your chosen fabric colours directly onto the corresponding pieces of the foundation paper. If you do this for several pieces at the beginning of a unit, it will help to it keep clear in your mind which piece belongs to which as you start the piecing sequence.

■ Foundation piecing produces a mirror image of the drawn pattern you stitch along. This has been taken into consideration for the patterns in this book but worth thinking about when designing your own work.

■ All of the quilts shown in this book were quilted by machine except for the two made by Phoebe Bartleet, which were hand quilted. Most of them were quilted with a combination of straight line quilting and free motion quilting which is achieved with the feed dogs lowered. In-the-ditch quilting is straight line quilting along a seam with the line of stitches falling on the lower side of the seam where the seam allowance has been pressed to the other side. Whether you quilt by hand or machine is personal choice. Information on how each quilt was quilted is given at the end of each pattern but these are only suggestions.

■ The methods in this book use pieces which are cut out a bit larger than the pattern piece for which they will be used. In the cutting instructions for each quilt you will be given the measurements for these pieces. These measurements include the seam allowances and also a small amount to allow for ease when piecing. Everyone works in

a different way and you may find you want more or less of an allowance for ease. Make a trial block before cutting out all the pieces for a quilt. If the size of the pieces suit you, carry on with the same size pieces. If not, make adjustments to the cutting measurements for the foundation pieces before cutting out further blocks. Most quilters will find the allowances given with the patterns to be adequate.

■ The quilts in this book use pieces cut to a given size for the foundation piecing. However, they could just as easily be made using strips cut to a certain width with the strip being trimmed off as you add each new piece. I prefer to work with pieces rather than strips because it is less cumbersome and allows me to chain piece with comfort. Using strips to foundation piece may be more comfortable for some people and this is another good reason for making a trial block. The amount of fabric required can sometimes be less when piecing with strips. If you are short of a certain fabric, consider using strips instead of pieces.

■ When designing your own patterns you will need to determine the size of the pieces to cut for foundation piecing. To do this, measure the width and length of the finished piece. Measure through the longest and the widest part of the piece. To each of those measurements, add a good inch for seam allowances and also for ease when piecing.

■ After sewing a seam which is longer than about 5", a better result will be obtained if the stitching line is pressed flat before being pressed to one side. This helps the resulting seam to be straighter and is particularly helpful when strip piecing.

■ When designing your own patterns, you will need to be figuring out the piecing order as you plan the design. With straight seams it is possible to sew seams which have paper foundations on both layers. You cannot, however, sew a curved seam sucessfully if there is a paper foundation on both layers. There is usually a way to get around it, as I did when sewing the two rings together in the Really Sharp Piecing block. Try to think of a way which won't end up loosing the wonderfully sharp points that you piece on paper. This is the reason for sewing the outer ring into the background before joining the two rings together.

■ Paper piecing is sewn with a very short stitch length to make the removal of the paper easier. Remember to revert to a normal stitch length for sewing seams which are not foundation pieced as it will make removing the stitches easier if you should make a mistake.

■ Even the most experienced foundation piecer gets it wrong from time to time. In workshops, and certainly from my own work, I have found that there are a handful of common errors when using these methods. They do not happen because you lack ability but rather because of the repetitive nature of the work. Yes, in the beginning perhaps you will make those errors as a result of being unsure. Later you will still make those errors occasionally because the work is methodical and the mind wanders. The fact that the mind can wander means that the technique is, on the whole, relaxing.

Seam ripping is never a popular activity and certainly not when it is foundation stitched using a very short stitch length. Often the paper foundation becomes torn in the process. Tape any tears with clear tape as soon as they appear. A clear tape will allow you to see the stitching lines.

I use a method of undoing paper pieced stitching which rarely causes any damage and once you get used to doing it, is extremely quick and easy. Best of all, no longer do I dread these inevitable mistakes.

You need a small pair of scissors with really sharp points. Lay the foundation unit down on a table with the paper side down. Work the edge of the piece that you need to remove free by using the scissors to snip at the first stitches. The stitching will start outside of the seam lines and usually outside of the cutting lines and therefore, if you should nick the fabric when loosening the edge it will not matter; it will be cut off when you are trimming the pieced unit. Using the hand without the scissors, lift the loosened edge and then whilst holding this up, use the scissors in the other hand to take small snipping "bites". These bites will just nick the stitches which become visible as you lift the top piece. As one hand is holding the piece to be removed taut to reveal the stitches, the other hand takes a tiny snip with

*Figure 101*

the scissors. Then use the tip of the scissors to hold the unit down onto the table as the other hand gives a little tug to reveal more stitches *(Figure 101)*.

Continue this for the length of the offending seam. Remove the loose threads from the foundation unit. As for the piece you removed, simply use the opposite edge of it as the stitching line and reapply it. You must use small, sharp scissors and take care not to snip the fabrics as you work along the seam. When you get used to it, you will find it very quick indeed.

■ Removing the foundation paper is easy but not a particularly fun job. The quickest and easiest method of removing the paper is to do it in an ordered fashion. I always remove the $1/4$" seam line section before going on to the centre sections. Keep a pair of tweezers handy to pick out difficult bits. Take care not to distort your work by pulling at it when removing papers and after the paper is removed handle it with care. A quilt top can get badly stretched simply from the way it is handled before it is layered up for quilting.

■ Avoid designing heavily pieced foundation units which butt up against each other and share a common seam. The seam could be difficult to sew but the main problem would be dealing with the accumulated bulk along the seam. From experience, I have found that with two very heavily pieced sections the resulting seam is so unattractive as to be unacceptable. There is usually a way around it and this was the case when I was making Solstice. Originally, I designed it so that the curve with green spikes actually touched the spikes in the sashing. The seam was very disappointing and so I inserted a strip of plain red fabric between the two heavily pieced units. Not only did it cure the problem but it also forced me to reverse the positions of the red and the orange in the sashing. This in turn strengthened the overall design.

■ When cutting out photocopied templates which have curved edges, you may find it easier if you use a small rotary cutter. The smaller blade will go around the curve better, especially on tighter curves.

■ If at anytime when foundation piecing you are unsure whether the piece you have added will be large enough, just hold it up to the light. Look at it from the pattern side. You can see the fabric through the paper and tell if it will be large enough to cover the piece it is intended for including seam allowances. Once in a while, a seam allowance that is as small as $1/8$" is fine.

# DESIGN

When I first started working on this book, the plan was to present a book of patterns using my techniques for foundation piecing. I knew these methods had a lot of scope for design possibilities, but I did not realise just how endless these possibilities were until I began actively designing the quilts for this book. This made me aware that I wanted quilters to use the techniques, explore the possibilities and come up with their own original and exciting designs. This chapter is not intended as a comprehensive guide to pattern drafting; there are already many excellent books covering that subject. My intention is to start you off thinking in new directions, finding new and exciting ways to use foundation piecing.

The best way to start exploring this type of design work is to take a pencil in hand and make loads of rough doodles. As you read this chapter, do so with a pencil and paper to hand. Continually let your pencil discover "what if" by adding new lines or sometimes by taking lines away. Don't be concerned about the quality or accuracy of your rough drawings. That is exactly what they are - rough! However, they serve their purpose and allow you to very quickly develop ideas. At least three-quarters of the rough sketches will come to nothing. Either you won't like the design or find it boring or discover that the piecing sequence is not suitable for this foundation method. Every so often you will hit upon a real gem that you just cannot wait to start piecing. This is the time to make an accurate pattern.

I am very fortunate in that my husband, Peter, is very willing and able to draw up my designs for me on the computer. If you are able, or know someone who is able to draw your designs by computer then that is the obvious answer. However, most people are likely to draft their designs by hand and there is certainly nothing wrong with that.

*Figure 201* shows a grid which would be used for designing. This grid has been printed full-size on the pattern sheets which are in the back pocket of the book. It is labeled Design Grid and will get you started drafting your own patterns. Looks can be deceiving and from what appears to be a rather simple grid of radiating lines and concentric circles you can produce some surprisingly complicated designs. The radiating lines are spaced five degrees apart, making 72 lines in the 360 degree circle. The circles are $1/4$" apart. All of the blocks for quilts in this book, except for the Solstice block, can be drawn using this grid. It is so easy to use the grid that it could be compared to drawing dot-to-dot.

The following six drawings show just how straightforward it is to draw a pattern for a 2-ring design using the grid. A 2-ring design consists of a centre and two rings of piecing. In *Figure 202*, you can see the grid with three circles drawn on it. The smallest circle indicates the edge of what will become the appliquéd centre. The middle circle shows the edge of the inner ring and the largest circle indicates the edge of the outer ring. For clarity, the

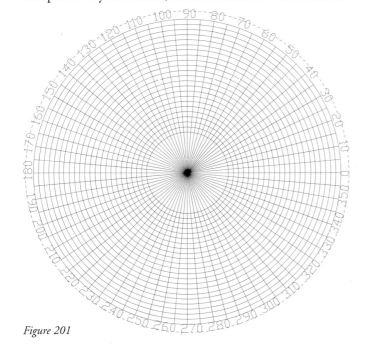

*Figure 201*

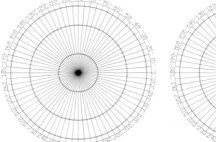

*Figure 202*

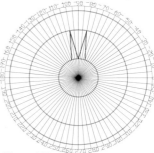

*Figure 203*

rest of the circles printed on the Design Grid have been

omitted. Points are made by drawing angled lines between the circles at regularly spaced intervals. In *Figure 203*, you can see the first two points drawn. The inner ring is completed in *Figure 204* by continuing around to form a ring with eighteen points.

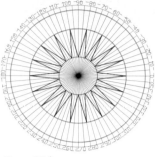

*Figure 204*

The number of points that you are able to put into a ring depends on the number of radiating lines in the grid. The number of radiating lines in the grid must be evenly divisible by the number of points that you want in your ring. The are 72 radiating lines in this grid and 18 points in the ring meaning that a point is formed on every fourth radiating line.

By following exactly the same procedure in *Figures 205* and *206*, the outer ring is drawn, also with eighteen points.

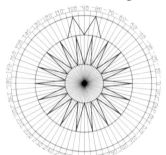

*Figure 205*

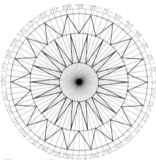

*Figure 206*

The circles on the grid are $1/4$" apart and make adding seam allowances easy. *Figure 207* shows the Really Sharp Piecing Block with it's seam allowances added and ready for use.

By placing a square over the grid, *Figure 208*, you could draw square blocks of the sort used in Columns, on page 52. The method of drawing would be the same as for circles only this time the edge of the outer "ring" would be square. Other shapes can also be used with this grid and hopefully, as you go through the rest of this chapter, you will start to come up with ideas of your own.

To use the grid, either get photocopies of it made or use masking tape to hold tracing paper in place and draw over it. Do not draw directly on

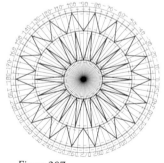

*Figure 207*

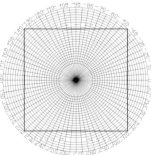

*Figure 208*

the original grid. The tracing paper has an advantage in that when you are finished with the drawing it will not have all of the radiating lines on it and can be photocopied to produce very clear patterns. If using tracing paper, it is a good idea to trace the circles using a compass to get really smooth lines. When drawing your lines, use a sharp pencil to get fine lines which will produce really sharp points when sewn. I find a mechanical pencil works best for this. A good ruler with tapered edges for drawing will enable you to work accurately.

When using the grid yourself, you will be able to decide the size and number of circles to use, how many points, as well as the shape of the overall design. A lot of choices to make, but then that's what designing is all about and the choice is always yours.

The quilts presented in this book are basically foundation pieced. There is nothing new about foundation piecing. It has been in use since the early days of quiltmaking. Then, it was used mainly as a method of easily using up small bits of fabric, usually in a crazy quilting type of formation or in string pieced shapes. Now, more and more, it is used to achieve an amazing degree of accuracy. Using my methods, even a relative beginner can produce highly complex quilts, very accurately, with ease. What is new about my method is that it allows you to go the full circle with foundation piecing. You can also piece very long straight units for borders which are stable and of an exact measurement. The points will be spot on every time whether the strip is made up of spikes or of the triangles in bias squares. Curved units can take on new and interesting shapes.

## RING DESIGNS

In the past, you had to look at a pattern and determine if it could be foundation pieced based on whether or not it had a logical foundation piecing order and if it had a beginning and an ending. Many designs simply cannot be successfully foundation pieced because of areas where seams intersect or come to a T-junction. Foundation piecing of quarter circle blocks as well as many other blocks has been in common use for a very long time. They have been readily viewed as successful candidates for

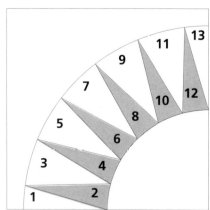

foundation or paper piecing because they have an obvious starting and stopping place. The quarter circle blocks have also been sewn together to form circles *(Figure 209)*.

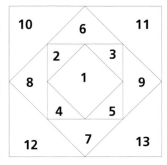

The problem with sewing the quarter circles together to form full circles is that that is exactly what it looks like - four quarter circle blocks sewn together. I'm not saying there's anything wrong with quarter circle blocks sewn together because many times it can be helpful to get a certain effect. At other times, the desired effect can only be achieved with a full circle. Full circles cannot be foundation pieced because the continuous nature of a circle will not allow for a beginning and an ending which is necessary for foundation piecing.

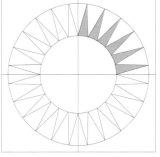

*Figure 209*

However, as shown by the quilts and the techniques in this book, you can cut into a circle thereby making a beginning and an ending, and later re-join it without compromising the accuracy.

Any shape that can be foundation pieced in a ring can be considered. Hexstar, on page 64, is an example of a hexagon shape which has been cut through, pieced in a ring and re-joined. Similarly, A Fishy Affair, on page 38, uses a square for the small sashing blocks.

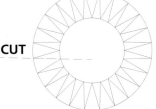

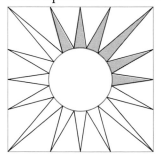 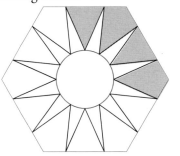

This same type of spiky star can be inserted into any number of shapes. Try putting it into a rectangle, an oval or a triangle.

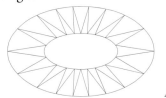 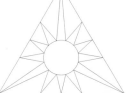

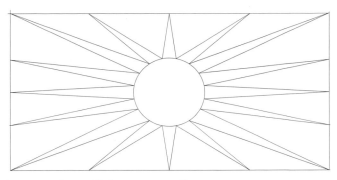

Try rounding off the corners of a square.

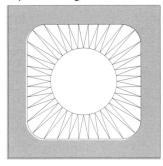 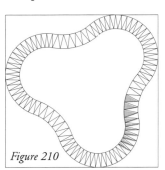

*Figure 210*

Any shape that can be pieced in a ring by cutting into it can be made with this technique. This means that the ring, whatever it's shape, will have to have a centre which will cover the inside edge of the pieced ring. Remember that the centre need not always be a circle and you could use any shape that compliments your design.

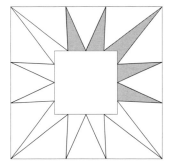 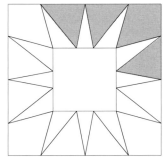

The more you work with this type of piecing, the quicker you will be able to get it clear in your mind whether a design can be foundation pieced. Basically, in order for a design to work, you have to be able to add to your "string" of piecing, whether it be a long, straight line of piecing or a curved unit, by adding on one piece at a time. Usually, this piece has to be one which is sewn with a line which goes through the foundation from edge to edge. A ring or strip of piecing which has a zigzag line running edge to edge will always work.

This zigzag line can be at any angle and could be used to make a star look as though it were spinning. Lines drawn straight through the

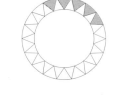

foundation can also be useful. The inner ring of Roll'em, Roll'em, Roll'em, on page 76, was designed with segments which were almost straight, producing a wedge shape rather than a spiky point. Try this with other shapes.

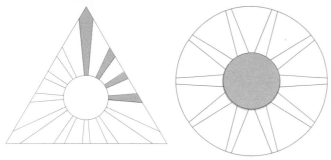

A very good motto when doodling for designs is "Let no shape go untried". Very often, the best and the most unusual designs develop from those that you'd originally thought not worth even trying out as a rough drawing. If you don't try it, you'll never know if it had possibilities.
I was playing with the rectangle once and came up with the block below which I'm sure has great potential for sashing in a quilt.

By using the techniques for 2-Ring Circular Piecing, on page 29, you will begin to think about joining more than two rings together to make up a design. The important thing to remember here is the order in which you sew the rings together. Follow the techniques for sewing the circles together but always start with the outer ring and work inwards. Working in this way, you can add as many rings as you wish. Size will probably be the limiting factor in most cases, *(Figure 211)*.
Try varying the width, and therefore the number, of points in the rings. The points in the outer ring could be slender and those in the inner ring wider. This would result in a greater number of points in the outer ring and less in the centre. The ring with more points will

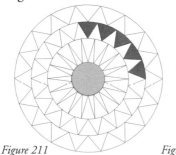

Figure 211

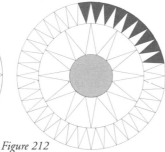

Figure 212

always be a multiple of the number in the ring with fewer points, *(Figure 212)*. 2-Ring Piecing is not limited to circles. Try it with other shapes as well.

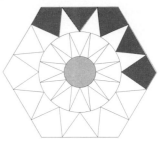

You could also try unconventional arrangements by working off-centre.

It is not a good idea to design rings of piecing which have points that meet when the rings are sewn together. Yes, it is possible, but it is much more difficult to get those points to come out really sharp because of the bulk where the seams all come together. When I designed Solstice, I had not devised the method of making it. In the sashing block *(Figure 213)*, I off-set the points as a design element. Luck was on my side for if I'd designed it with the points meeting, I probably

would have gone ahead and pieced it in the traditional way and never have come up with the idea of "Ring Piecing" at all.

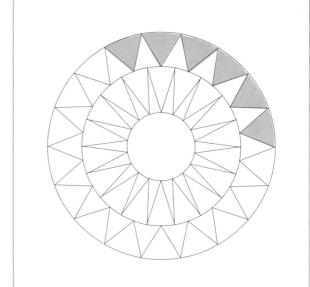

Figure 213

## CURVED UNIT PIECING

As I said earlier, foundation piecing of quarter circle units has been around for a very long time. Don't limit your thinking to these. In the large Solstice block *(Figure 214)*, I used two curved units in the same block. One was the straightforward quarter circle and the other a larger, exaggerated arc. When designing curved unit blocks, remember to try two or more different curved units within one block.

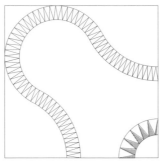

*Figure 214*

There are many possibilities for changing the shape of the curved unit. This is where you will have to do a lot of playing to find shapes which are pleasing to you.

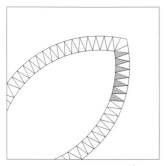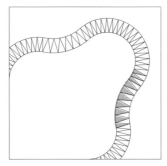

Try arranging the blocks into sets of four to see if any interesting shape emerges.

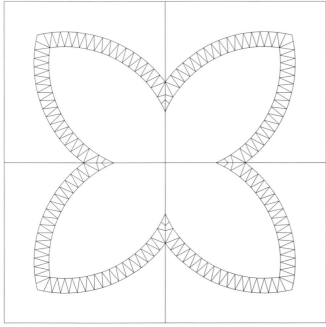

*Figure 215*

With both of these blocks you would have to consider how to deal with the areas of pieced units which meet when the blocks are sewn together. For the design in *Figure 215*, it would not be a major problem because there are not that

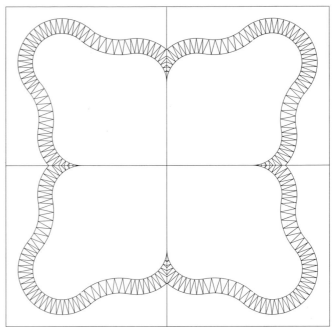

*Figure 216*

many seams involved and I would certainly consider this design feasible. As for the design in *Figure 216*, the bulk could prove a real problem if the blocks were left with this piecing arrangement. One possibility would be to eliminate some of the spikes at the end of each pieced unit, however, it may not be the look you're after.

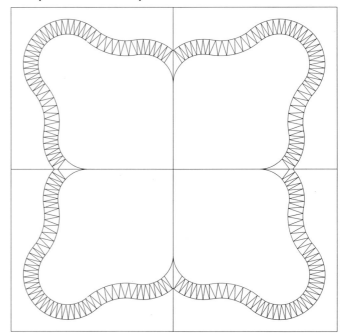

This could also be a problem when grouping blocks with ring units such as the one shown in *Figure 212*. Although the area of the seam line where the pieced units touch is short, it could still cause a very bulky seam, *(Figure 217)*. When you come across this type of problem try looking at an alternative setting. A narrow sashing strip through the middle would solve the problem for both of these designs and could in fact, strengthen the design by the introduction

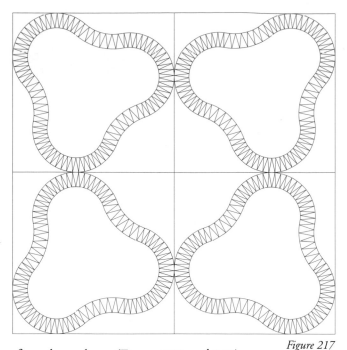

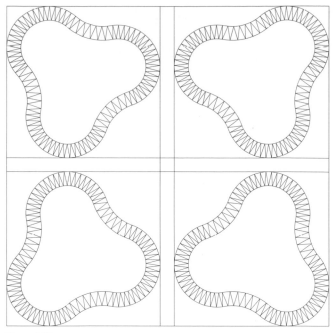

of another colour, *(Figures 218 and 219).*

*Figure 217*

*Figure 219*

Another solution to consider when this problem involves ring pieced blocks is to put a margin around the outside of the ring. From my experience, it also happens to be easier to sew a ring into a block which has a margin right the way around the ring, even if it is only a margin of say $^1/_4$"-$^1/_2$" wide. There would still be the seam allowance to add on

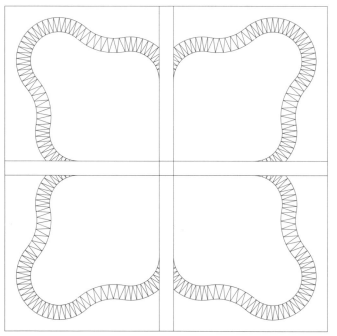

and this would make it possible to work with as little as a $^1/_4$" margin.

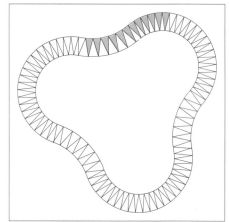

*Figure 218*

Design work should be fun and one of the most enjoyable aspects of quiltmaking. If you think, "I'll never come up with my own original designs", then you're wrong! That is exactly what I used to think and have come to realise that nothing ventured is nothing gained, and being afraid to even roughly sketch a design will get you nowhere. Yes, there will be times when you come up with ideas which at first will seem impossible to make into a quilt. When designing, whether it be quilts, clothing or even motor cars, a great deal of time is usually spent problem solving. Each time you solve a problem, you strengthen your abilities and become ready to accept even greater challenges.

*Untitled* - 17" x 17" - Barbara Barber   1997

*Really Sharp Piecing Blocks* - 22" x 22" - Shirley Shotton, Oxford, England   1997

*Lilac Feathers* - 90" x 90" - Barbara Barber, Hampshire, England   1996

*Really Sharp Piecing Block* - 18" x 18"
Maggie Barber,
London, England   1997

*Really Sharp Piecing Block* - 18" x 18"
Julie Standen,
Bristol, England   1996

*Really Sharp Piecing Block* - 18" x 18"
Lois Andrews,
Surrey, England   1996

*Really Sharp Piecing Block* - 18" x 18"
Shelagh Jarvis,
London, England   1996

*Really Sharp Piecing Block* - 18" x 18"
Linda Park,
London, England   1997

*Really Sharp Piecing Block* - 18" x 18"
Sylvia Vance,
E. Sussex, England   1997

*Good Morning Sunshine* - 108" x 108" - Phoebe Bartleet, Hampshire, England   1996

**Rolled'em, Rolled'em, Rolled'em**
**- Too Far**
69" x 94$\frac{1}{4}$"
Myra Ibbetson,
Dorset, England    1996

**Really Sharp Piecing Block** - 18" x 18"
Linda Park, London, England    1997

**Untitled** - 42" x 42"
Angela Hodge,
Hertfordshire,
England    1997

**Unquilted**
Sarah Hadfield, Nottinghamshire, England    1997

*Untitled* - 15" x 15"
Myra Ibbetson, Dorset, England    1996

*Untitled* - 75" x 75" - Shirley Bolt, Hampshire, England    1997

*Christmas Cats* - 65" x 112"
Veronica Gilberts, Worcestershire, England    1997

*Unquilted* - 50" x 50" - Sally Laine, Hampshire, England    1997

*Goato & Friends* - 83" x 83" - Barbara Barber, Hampshire, England   1995
Collection of the Museum of the American Quilter's Society, Paducah, Kentucky, USA.
*Photo courtesy of American Quilter's Society*

# THE TECHNIQUES

## PHOTOCOPIES

Photocopies are readily available in this country in two sizes - A4 (standard page) and A3 (two standard pages). Photocopies larger than these are available but not all that easy to obtain. The designs printed within the pages of the book can be made on A4 copies but those which are folded into the back pocket will require the A3 size. A lot of the designs are even larger than the A3 size but that is not a problem. All of the designs are symmetrical and therefore, if you copy half of the block onto an A3 sheet of paper and glue two of these copies together you will get a full-sized design sheet.

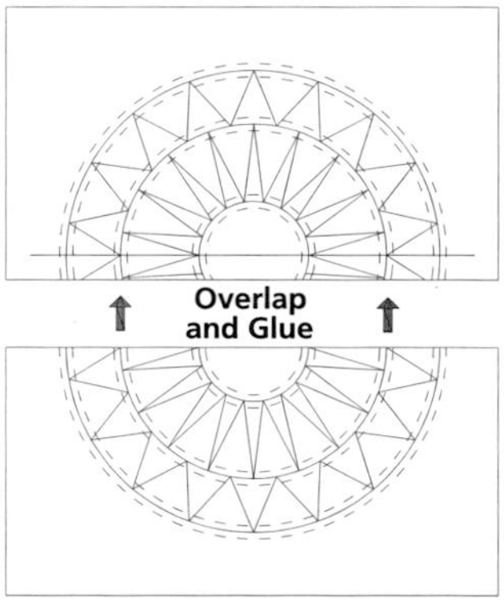

Trim away any more than about 1" overlap in the centre of the design to alleviate the double thickness of paper as much as possible. You can easily align the pattern lines and glue the two sheets together using a light box but I've found that if you work on a plain white surface - I use

the reverse side of one of the copies - you can usually line up the pattern and glue it without using either a light box or holding it up onto a window. Although it may seem a bit tricky at first, you'll soon find that you are able to glue them accurately and quickly. The best place to start when gluing is in the centre of the design and work out in one direction to the edge. Then go back to the centre and work out to the other edge, carefully aligning the pattern as you go.

When gluing together copies of straight units I always overlap the copies by one whole square or triangle of the design. This may mean that I use

slightly more copies but it will also mean that the finished unit will be more accurate. The beauty of using this method of piecing a long border of bias squares or triangles is that the finished measurement is certain to be exactly what you intended it to be. When gluing together copies that make

up a long section, I always number the individual pieces by writing directly on the copies as I glue them together. Always double check the numbering sequence and also be sure to carefully compare the prepared foundation to the section of the quilt you are making.

The cutting out of the photocopies is detailed with each different technique in this chapter. Do not cut your copies until you have read the instructions for the technique you are using.

If the section or block you want to copy is very large, you may like to consider finding a copier that can make even larger copies. This is what I did when making Solstice, on page 84, as the blocks in this quilt measure $21^5/8$" square. On the other hand, you don't have to use very large copies to make Solstice. Smaller copies of overlapping sections of the block could be glued together to form the pattern for the whole block. It is important that the copies overlap by at least an inch to ensure an accurate pattern.

Before making loads of copies for a quilt, make just one copy of a pattern and compare it to the original for distortion. You are likely to get a small amount of distortion on even the best photocopier and therefore it is a good idea to make all your copies on the same machine. Photocopy machines are very good these days and the small amount of distortion has never been a problem for me. Sometimes I have obtained the best results by setting the copier to 99%. This is usually for long, narrow patterns.

After you have found a good copier, get just enough copies to make one block. This block may just be a sample to test out colour or may become part of the quilt. By making just enough copies for one block you are able to try it out. You will see if you like the look of it and enjoy sewing it enough to make the whole quilt. Usually you will be so pleased with the fine sharp points you've achieved that you can't wait to start on the whole quilt. This is the time to return to the same photocopier and get the required number of copies you need to complete the quilt. I always get spare copies to allow for the odd mistake. Most importantly, ALWAYS make your copies from the original pattern. Copies from a copy will lead to a very distorted pattern and a very disappointing result.

Instead of getting copies made, you could, of course,

Inside the diagram (top of left column):

**↑ Overlap and Glue ↑**

trace the design. This would be quite time consuming for a whole quilt but not such a problem for a single block. If you do opt for tracing, take care to do it accurately as a successful outcome depends on an accurate pattern. Again, ALWAYS trace from the original pattern.

## UNDERSTANDING THE FULL-SIZE PATTERNS

In the Introduction, I said, "EXPECT TO BE CONFUSED". I also said, "IT WILL ALL SUDDENLY BECOME CLEAR" - and it will! Understanding the full-size foundation pattern as drawn can be, and usually is, confusing. Once you are able to view a drawn pattern in the correct way, there is no problem with understanding further patterns. The full-size patterns printed in this book are usually presented as a whole design, rather than with separate templates. The designs could have been printed with all of the sections of the pattern separated, although it would have made a very bulky book. The reason for printing the designs as a whole is because it is actually part of the overall technique and does, in fact, make things easier once you understand how to "read" the design. Also, I feel you will want to be able to use the methods to design and make your own original quilts. When drawing and making your own designs, this system of incorporating the seam allowances into the pattern drawn as a whole will make it quicker, easier and much more accurate.

When you first look at a full-size pattern which involves circular or curved units, you may think it looks like a maze of lines, whilst the straight line units have only one set of lines to define the pattern with no added seam allowances drawn. All *cutting lines* in this book are drawn with a **broken** or **dotted line**. All **solid lines** on the full-size patterns are *seam lines*. To use the methods successfully, you must get it clear in your mind which seam allowances belong to which unit or piece and why. The patterns for these techniques are, in a sense, piled up one on top of another. The seam allowances for one section may, therefore, be printed on part of another section. The paper foundations are cut apart in order to paper piece the individual sections. When piecing a certain section you will often have the dotted seam allowance from another section shown on the section you are piecing. You must come to recognise which seam allowances belong to which sections and learn to ignore them when they appear inside of a section you are piecing. If a dotted line is *within* a certain section, it will not actually have anything to do with that section. Seam allowances for any piece or section will always be *outside* of the seam line for that area. For any piece or unit, there has to be ¼" seam allowance beyond the drawn seam line. On curved designs, it is easier to

draw this on as part of the pattern and then use this dotted line to trim the unit after piecing. On straight units it is easier to simply add the ¼" to the solid seam line when trimming the completed unit. Cutting the paper foundations, piecing and trimming are detailed later in this chapter.

*Figure 401* shows a Really Sharp Piecing block in its completed form. In *Figure 402*, you see the same block

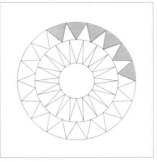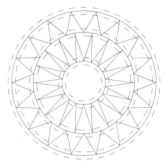

Figure 401                    Figure 402

with all of the cutting lines included. This is the way this block would be printed, full-size, for you to work from. Look at the drawing and try to analyse which seam allowances belong to which sections. As you read through the techniques, you will see that a lot of the designs are made using "Ring Piecing" or "Curved Units". The circular block above is made up of four sections. For this type of piecing you must learn to recognise the different sections of a design and the seam lines which will sew the different sections together.

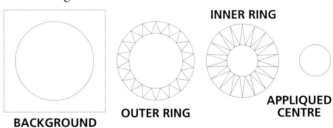

INNER RING

OUTER RING

APPLIQUED CENTRE

BACKGROUND

Each one of these sections have one line in common with the next and that line is the seam line used to join the sections together. Naturally, each of these sections will require a seam allowance in order to sew them together to make the whole. These seam allowances will extend ¼" beyond each seam line.

In order to sew the pieced section of the design into the background square, a hole or circle of the correct size has to be cut out from the background fabric. You could make a square template with a hole of the correct size in the middle. It would look like *Figure 403*. An easier way would be to make a freezer paper template which is the size of the hole you need to cut out. Usually templates are made for pieces which will be included in a block, however, on this occasion the freezer paper template will be made for a piece that will not actually be used in the block. This template will be for the hole that is cut out and must allow for the background fabric to have a $1/4$" seam allowance on the inside of the solid seam line. The template would be made using the inner dotted line in *Figure 403* as the cutting line. After using a freezer paper template to cut out the hole you will have a fabric square which will look like *Figure 403* except, of course, that the seam allowances would not be drawn onto the fabric. Full information is given in the piecing sections of this chapter about making the template and cutting out the circle. At this point, concentrate on understanding what all of the lines on the pattern mean.

*Figure 403*

The outer ring will be pieced onto a paper foundation that has been cut through. It will be foundation pieced as a long, curving strip and then re-joined into a full circle. Seam allowances are required both inside and outside of this ring in order to sew this ring to the other sections of the block. The dotted lines which are $1/4$" beyond the inside and outside edges of the pieced ring will be the trimming line after you have completely pieced the ring. This will add the necessary $1/4$" seam allowances to the ring.

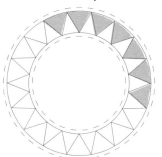

*Figure 404*

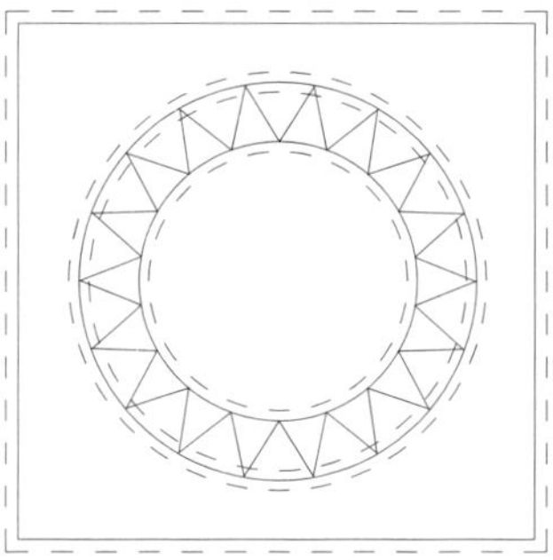

*Figure 405*

*Figure 405* shows the outer ring, including its cutting lines, placed on top of the background square with its cutting lines. It is easy to understand that in order for the finished block to measure 18" square, the background fabric must be cut $18^1/_2$" x $18^1/_2$" to allow for the seams around the outside of the block. The circular patterns in this book use squares of a stated size for the backgrounds. You can rotary cut a square of any given size, including the seam allowances, without using a template. Therefore, the square, drawn with its seam allowances, is not a necessary part of the full-size pattern. All of the other lines are necessary. *(Figure 406)*. Get it clear in your mind what each of the lines is used for before going further. At this stage, don't worry about the piecing of the ring as this will be explained in

detail later in this chapter. The inner ring will be dealt with in the same way as the outer ring. The inner ring is shown in *Figure 407* with the seam allowances added to the outer and inner edges.

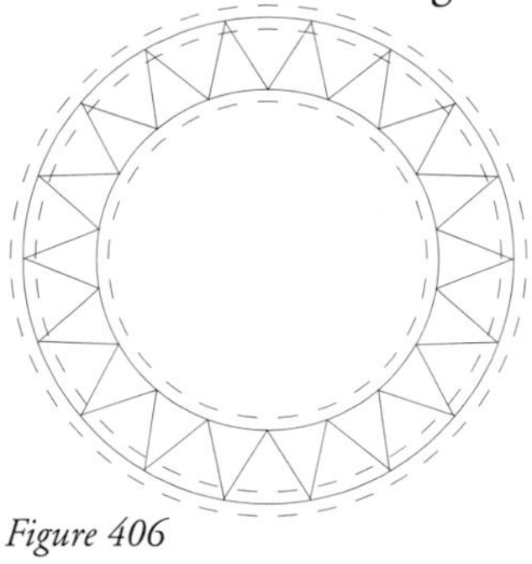

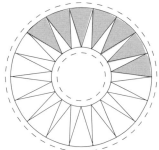

*Figure 406*

*Figure 407*

This section of the drawing can now be placed on top of the previous drawing of the outer ring with its seam allowances included. The appliquéd centre will need a seam allowance added around the outside of it *(Figure 409)*.

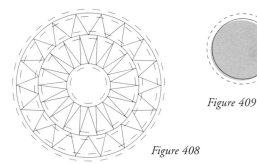

*Figure 409*

*Figure 408*

This centre section should be added to the rest of the drawing. This pattern is now complete and ready for use.

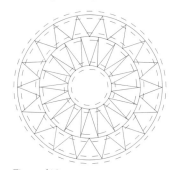

*Figure 410*

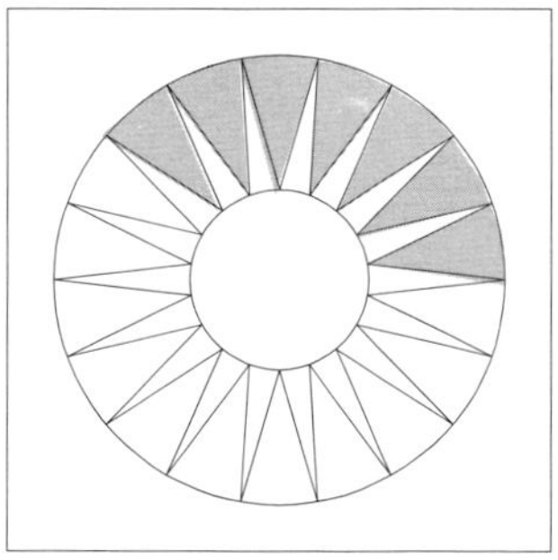

*Figure 411*

There may be times when you want to make a block using only the inner ring of a design. This is the case with the quilt, Scarecrows & Reindeer, on page 80. There is no need for a whole new drawing - simply utilize the parts of the drawing that you need. Shown below is the drawing that would be necessary to make that block. The template for cutting the hole out from the background square would now be made

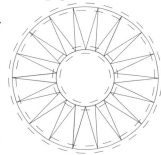

*Figure 414*

using the second dotted line in from the outside edge.

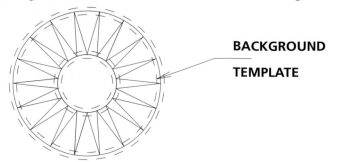

BACKGROUND

TEMPLATE

The pattern for a block which is made using Curved Unit Piecing can be dealt with in the same way. *Figure 412* shows a block from the quilt, Autumn Forest, on page 42.

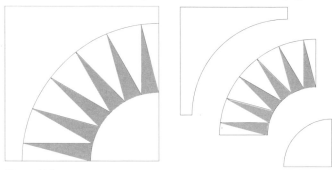

*Figure 412*

Look at this block and define the three separate sections of it. If you added the seam allowances to the individual units, this is how they would look. Add those cutting lines to the block as a whole unit. The pattern for this block would be presented for use with all necessary seam allowances included.

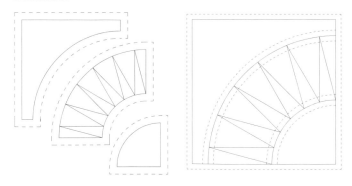

This "piling up" of the pattern is a great help and was not thought up simply as a means of saving space in the book. When I first devised the method for piecing Solstice, this "piling up" system was part of it from the start. The reason then was accuracy. It's still a good enough reason for me. There is far less scope for inaccuracy if the design is only drawn once. Also, it can be helpful, sometimes, in reducing the number of photocopies you require because sometimes it is possible to use one photocopy for two different parts of the design. In 2-Ring blocks, you can use one photocopy for both the outer ring and the appliquéd

centre. This is because these sections are not touching each other and therefore, you can cut them apart and use them separately. The same applies to the Autumn Forest block above. From one copy of this block you can use both the D and C pieces for templates as they do not touch each other. Another very good reason for using this "piling up" method is that it provides automatic positioning marks which are extremely useful when piecing the sections together. This will be explained with the piecing.

With an understanding of seam lines and cutting lines, you will be able to apply the same techniques to patterns that you have designed and drawn. Take great care when adding the $1/4$" seam allowances to your own drawings and you should have no trouble in sewing them together. After all, your pattern was whole and fitted together properly before you cut it up to piece the units.

The full-size patterns for designs which have Straight Unit Piecing are easier to understand. They will not include the broken or dotted cutting line and therefore, do not include seam allowances.

## PHOTOCOPIED TEMPLATES

In my work, I try to use measurements to cut out pieces with the rotary cutter and ruler if at all possible. This is, undoubtedly, the most accurate way but sometimes the pieces are oddly shaped or have curved edges which make this impossible. The simplest method I have found is to use photocopies as templates. I started using these methods in 1993 for a quilt which was extremely intricately pieced. It was not foundation pieced and therefore, accurate cutting of the pieces was vital to a successful outcome. I was delighted with the result and have been using this method ever since. When I started teaching it, students also found it an invaluable technique. The method may seem a little odd but it does work. Not only that, but it is incredibly easy and very quick.

In a nutshell, you staple photocopies onto strips of fabric and cut them out with a rotary cutter. I have never experienced any problems with the stapling and it does not damage the cotton fabrics usually used in quiltmaking. This method should not be used with thin or delicate fabrics. If you don't wish to use a stapler, you could tack the paper templates onto the fabric strips in the same way using a large stitch on the sewing machine. This was, in fact, the way I did it when I first started using this method. The stapling came about when I wanted to use larger templates and found that it was difficult to keep the paper template truly flat on the fabric under the sewing machine. For very large templates, such as the H and L pieces in

Solstice on page 84, I make a freezer paper template as detailed in the "2-Ring Circular Piecing" section of this chapter.

For most templates the stapling works well. As an example, I am going to work with the template labeled "Azdaz G", on page 46. Remember, in this book, all seam lines are drawn with a solid line and all cutting lines are shown with dotted lines on all full-size patterns. As you can see, the seam allowances are not included on the template. The pieces will be cut from a strip. Generally speaking with this method, you simply measure the template at its widest point, not including seam allowances, and add an inch. This inch will allow for $^1/_4$" seam allowance either side. The rest will be excess which I have found to be necessary for a good result. This is because the pieces are rotary cut and you need to have something to cut off to get a nice clean, accurate result. However, with oddly shaped pieces such as the Azdaz G piece, it is often a good idea to lay out a number of the templates to determine the most economical width to cut the strips. Cut out copies of the template; do not cut them out on the seam line but cut them out roughly about $^3/_8$" larger than the template on all sides. Lay them out to determine the width to cut the strips. In this instance, I decided that $8^1/_2$" would be the best width to cut the strips. They can be positioned closely together but do not make them share

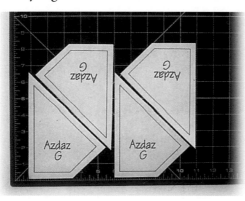

cutting lines. Estimate the number of strips you will need in order to be able to cut out the number of pieces that you require with that template. Cut the strips and stack them up on top of each other. Eight layers is the maximum number I would suggest you use at one time although, of course, you could use less. Position a template copy on the strip and staple it on. To keep it stable, I staple it in two different places. When adding the second staple, make sure that the paper remains flat on the fabric and no fullness has been stapled in. Attach all of the templates for the strip in this way. When using starched fabric strips which are more than 5" wide, it is helpful to position the strips so that one long edge overhangs the edge of the table far enough to allow you to staple on the templates without having to lift the fabric. Not only is it easier this way but it will keep the

template lying flat on the fabric.

After stapling along one edge, turn the strips around and staple along the other edge. These templates will now be cut out using the rotary cutter and ruler. Remember, the template does not include seam allowances. Add the seam allowance to each side of the template as you cut by positioning the $^1/_4$" line of the ruler on the solid seam line of the template. Take extra care when positioning the ruler on the line. The result will be very accurately cut pieces including their seam allowances.

Always check the placement of the ruler several times, up and down the template, before cutting. Check this placement again after you have applied pressure on the ruler as the staples can make the ruler slip when this pressure is applied. Most of my students have been happy to deal with this problem once they have been made aware of it. However, the staples can cause the ruler to slip slightly and if this does prove a real problem, then you should consider stitching the templates onto the strips as mentioned earlier. I have attached small sand paper discs to my rotary rulers which are very helpful in preventing slippage in all of my rotary cutting. These discs are sold for this purpose in quilt shops or you could devise something similar yourself. Continue cutting out the pieces until you have cut out all the pieces from the strip. When cutting the pieces, be sure to hold the rotary cutter upright; if the cutter is held at an angle while you cut eight layers, the bottom pieces will end up being either smaller or larger than the top piece, depending on whether the cutter was angled towards or away from the ruler. If the cutter is held perpendicular to the ruler this will not be a problem.

When stapling, if you cannot reach to the centre of the fabric strip because it is wider than the stapler will reach, then work one template at a time. Staple and cut each template before stapling the next. This will make the stapling easier as you can approach the template from more sides. Another alternative is to avoid using strips altogether and simply cut over-sized pieces and stack them up before stapling on the template. You may find that you prefer to work with over-sized pieces all of the time rather than working with strips.

Leave the paper templates attached to the fabric pieces until you are ready to use those pieces. By doing this, you are protecting the pieces and making sure that they do not become stretched or distorted by handling. Also, it keeps the pieces very tidy and easy to find. When you are ready to remove the paper template, turn the pieces over so that you can lift the folded-over ends of the staple. Find a suitable metal object for this purpose. An old metal nail file works very well. Once you have opened out the prongs of the staple, turn the piece back over and lift out the staple using your chosen metal object. I always love admiring the beautifully cut pieces of fabric that result.

The paper templates can be re-used. If you do re-use them, be sure to place the $^1/_4$" line of the rotary ruler on the solid seam line as before. Do not try to line up the edge of the ruler with the edge of the paper. This often results in a sliver of paper, and thus a bit of the seam allowance, being cut off. The same applies to templates which have the seam allowances included on the drawing. Always use the seam line as a guide and place the $^1/_4$" line of the rotary ruler on it. The templates which have their seam allowances included are usually those which have curved lines somewhere on the piece. The $^1/_4$" seam allowance cannot be added to the seam line with the rotary ruler on curved lines.

When cutting out a piece that has a combination of straight and curved edges, the methods are mostly the same as those for cutting templates with all straight edges. I still cut strips and staple on the templates. Use fewer layers of fabric when cutting out curved pieces; four is the maximum I would recommend. When cutting out the paper templates to staple onto the strips, always cut the paper slightly larger than the dotted cutting line. With curved templates, it is

not a good idea to re-use the paper templates as you will not have this little bit of excess paper beyond the dotted line and would mean that you would be trying to accurately cut along an already cut edge of paper. I never find this particularly easy or satisfactory. After stapling the templates onto the fabric strips, cut the straight edges of the template first. Using the same methods as before, cut these edges with the $^1/_4$" line of the ruler on the solid seam line. I cut the curved seam with the rotary cutter and follow the dotted cutting line of the template, without using a ruler as a guide. This is the method Maggie Barber used for cutting the C and D pieces in her quilt, Sunny Side Up, on page 96. She said she found it a very easy way to cut out those oddly shaped pieces and did not find it a problem to cut them without using a ruler. It must be said, however, that GREAT care must be taken when doing it! Rotary cutters are one of the quilter's greatest friends but, unless used with continual care, can be very dangerous!! If you are in any way uncomfortable about cutting without the ruler, then simply cut on the dotted line using a pair of sharp scissors. If you do use scissors, it is probably a good idea to limit the number of layers to a maximum of two to ensure accuracy.

On pieces which have curved seams, always mark the fabric to show any positioning points which are on the pattern before removing the template from the cut out piece. These points will be the little "v-shapes" in the seam allowance. When adding a pieced foundation unit to a piece cut out with a template you will be able to match the points sewn on the foundation unit to the marks drawn on the fabric. To make the positioning marks, lift just the edge of the template and put a small mark in the seam allowance of the fabric.

If a template is larger than about 6" or 7" square, I would suggest that you use the freezer paper template method given on page 29. This will prevent any buckling that might occur with larger pieces. Solstice is  the only quilt pattern in this book which has pieces large enough to require freezer paper templates. Remember to include seam allowances when making freezer paper templates. The quilts which have circular designs will use freezer paper templates to cut a hole out of the background fabric as detailed in the next section.

## 2-RING CIRCULAR PIECING

As the name implies, this technique is used for blocks which have two pieced rings. If, at anytime, you feel unsure about what the lines on the full-size pattern mean, refer back to "Understanding The Full-Size Patterns", earlier in this chapter. For my examples, I am going to work with the Really Sharp Piecing Design but the methods apply to all 2-ring designs.

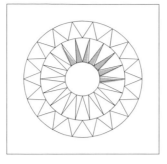

## FREEZER PAPER TEMPLATE

The first thing to do is to make a freezer paper template which can then be used to cut a hole out of the background square. Usually a template is made for a pattern piece which will be used to make up a block. In this instance, the template is made for a piece that is not going to be used in the block. The template is only used as a method of making sure that the correct size hole is cut out of the background fabric.

The **cutting line** for this template will be the *second dotted line* in from the outside edge of the design. In other words, the cutting line is the dotted line which is ¼" inside the largest solid circular line. A hole cut out of the background square using this template will allow for the necessary seam allowance for the curved seam. Cut out the design slightly larger than the dotted cutting line. Glue the wrong side of this copy onto the non-shiny side of the freezer paper. Now cut the copy which is glued to freezer paper exactly on the dotted cutting line. If you are doing it correctly, you will be cutting off just the tips of the points in the outer ring. Notice that there are four small lines which mark the quarter points of the circle.

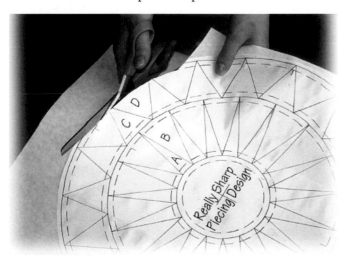

Make a pinhole in the template by inserting a pin through the crossed lines which indicate the very centre of the design.

The background square should be cut to the size of the finished block plus ½" for seam allowances. The quilt patterns in this book tell you to cut out squares of certain measurements; these will always include the seam allowances. I spray starch the background fabrics as well as those used inside of the block. Fold the square in half and crease along the fold by finger pressing. Unfold and then fold in half in the other direction, creasing on the fold as before. The reason for doing this is to find the exact centre of the square. Insert a straight pin through the right side of the fabric in the very centre point of the square. Now insert this pin through the pin hole made earlier in the centre of the template; enter the pin from the reverse, through the shiny side first. Holding the pin upright, place

the fabric square and template onto an ironing surface. Turn the template around on the pin to match up the quarter marks of the template to the folds you creased into the fabric square. Be sure to check for correct orientation as you position the template for each of the blocks in a quilt. In some blocks, a point falls at each quarter mark and thus, needs no special positioning. The Really Sharp Piecing block has points on only two of the quarter marks. After positioning, use the iron and continue to apply heat until the template is attached to the fabric. Remove the pin.

Use the same techniques for making the freezer paper templates when making half and quarter blocks for quilts like Roll'em, Roll'em, Roll'em, on page 76. Be sure to add the seam allowance to the straight edge where you cut the circle into a half or a quarter.

In order to position the pieced ring within the block, you will need to mark the background square. Going

around the edge of the template, mark each of the points of the design onto the background square. These are indicated by the tips which you cut off to make this template.

Generally, I use a pencil for this and make one small mark - about ⅛" long - to indicate each point. If the colour or pattern of the fabric is dark, I may use coloured pencils in order to be able to see the marks. Carefully cut around the template, cutting as close to the template as possible without cutting it. I make a slit in the fabric using my rotary cutter which is large enough to get the scissors through and then cut around with the scissors. Put the square to one side while you piece the block, taking care not to stretch the bias edges of the circle. As for the fabric circle that came out of the hole, well, I leave that to your imagination! It will not be used in the block but I have had many a student come up with wonderful uses for these perfect circles. The template can be used over and over until it will no long adhere to the fabric. This will vary depending on the freezer paper. I made both A Fishy Affair, on page 38, and Geoff & The Bears, on page 56, with just one freezer paper template.

## PIECING THE OUTER RING

Use one of the photocopies to cut out the outer ring for piecing *(Figure 404, page 25)*. Remember that you will need seam allowances extending $^1/_4$" beyond the seam lines on both the inside and the outside edges of the ring. If necessary, review "Understanding The Full-Size Patterns", earlier in this chapter. Do not cut exactly on the cutting line but roughly cut about $^1/_8$" beyond the cutting line; after piecing is complete you will trim the ring exactly on the cutting line. Don't be tempted to leave a larger margin or it will hinder your piecing. When cutting the middle out of the ring, avoid cutting into the centre circle; save the centre section of the copy to use when appliquéing the centre circle. Cut the ring open by carefully cutting on one of the solid seam lines of the points in the ring.

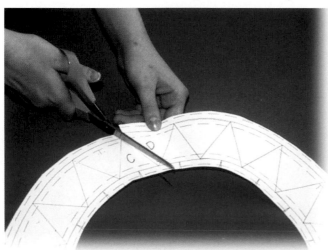

It does not matter which line you cut.

If you are making a quilt which has some half-blocks in it, such as Hexstar, on page 64, the block pattern will be printed with a solid line going through the centre of the

block. This central solid line is the seam line for the edge of the half-blocks. When cutting through the ring on these blocks be sure to cut through on a seam line for a point and not on the half-block seam line.

This ring is long and difficult to handle. In its present state it will slow you down and could easily get torn apart during the piecing. To avoid these problems, I piece long units, straight or curved, using a scroll method. Roll the pattern up with the printed design on the inside. Leave about 5" free at the end of the roll. I secure it by pinning with a long hefty straight pin through all the layers and this works well for me. Insert the pin on the inside of the roll to keep it from catching as you work. If you find it difficult to push the pin through, use an over-sized paper clip instead. After I have added several pieces, I unroll a bit more and continue. I never have more than about 5" of the unit unrolled at anytime because as soon as the pieced end is long enough, I start rolling it up in the same way forming a scroll. This way it stays neat and tidy and I find it a pleasant way to work, producing good results. Also, it allows me to chain piece up to 15 or 16 units at a time without them getting all tangled up.

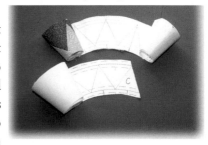

Put the pieces you cut for the outer ring in a handy position for piecing at the machine. Set your stitch size to about 1.5 or about 20 stitches per inch. Establish clearly in your mind which cut piece belongs to the pieces printed on the paper ring. In my example, the first piece could have been either the C or the D piece. It happens to be a C piece. This will depend on where the ring was cut through. You may find it helpful to write the piece letter and the fabric colour onto the foundation paper for the first few pieces of the ring.

Pick up one of each of the cut fabrics. They will probably be different sizes regardless of what design you are making. Their lengths may be the same but their widths will probably be different. Place them, right sides together, with the long edges even on one side. Lay them on your sewing machine extension table with the wrong side of the fabric which is the first in the ring on top. Position the rolled paper ring on these fabrics. The top fabric should be just a bit larger than the first piece of the pattern. The first solid line you see will be the first seam line. The seam allowance will be on the rolled side of the solid line. Position the foundation so that a scant $^1/_4$" of fabric lies beyond the solid line on the rolled side of the foundation. The ends of the fabric pieces should protrude just beyond the cut edges of the paper ring allowing you to position the fabric without having to hold it up to the light.

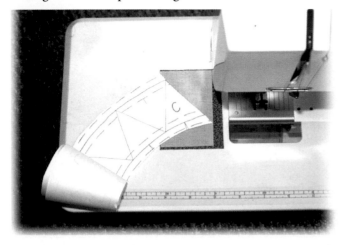

Hold the foundation firmly in place and slide over to stitch. Place it with the seam line straight in front of the needle. Lower the stitch size to produce smaller stitches – I use a 1.5 stitch length when paper piecing.

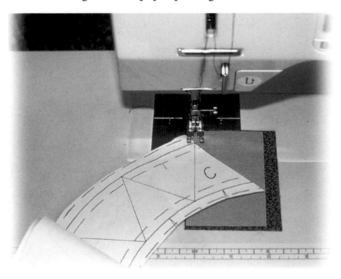

Sew from the very edge of the fabric right through to the other the other edge and remove from the machine. In *Figure 413*, you can see the front and back of this first seam. The two on the left show it as it is when removed from the machine. The middle ones show this same seam after it has been finger pressed open. On the right, the pieces have been trimmed and pressed. Trim the fabric very close to the curved edges of the ring. On the short end where you cut the ring open, trim the fabric to about 3/8". After you have finished piecing the ring, this will form the seam allowance when the ring is re-joined.

The first two pieces of a ring are always added in this way. All of the rest of the pieces in the ring are added in the following way.

The pieces are added in an alternating sequence. Place

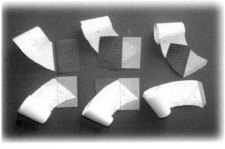

the correct fabric piece on the sewing machine extension table with the right side facing up. Position the next solid seam line over the fabric

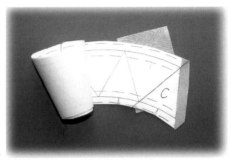

Figure 413

with a scant 1/4" seam allowance extending beyond the line towards the paper roll which has not yet been pieced. The larger part of this piece will be under the fabric you have already sewn.

I have found it very helpful to always work with the roll which has not been pieced placed in the same position on the sewing machine table. The roll of pattern which has not been pieced is always placed on my left hand side. This seems to help alleviate a few of those common mistakes I mentioned earlier and allows me to chain piece without getting muddled.

Sew this seam in the same way as the first and remove from the machine. Before opening the piece out, trim the seam allowances for the seam you have just sewn. It is important to trim the seam allowance to about 1/4" not only because it gives a better finish but also because with light coloured fabrics the darker one could show through. If you forget to trim the odd one, it can be trimmed after the paper is removed. Open the piece out and finger press. Trim the fabric off level with the edges of the paper and press with the iron.

Continue to add pieces in this way until you have completed the ring. Trim the seam allowance of the final piece in the same way as for the first piece *(Right Figure 413)*. Using scissors, cut exactly on the curved dotted cutting line around the outer and inner edges of the ring.

To accurately join the ring back into a full circle, insert a straight pin just off the paper through what will become the solid seam lines on the outer and inner curved edges; enter the pins from the paper side. The pins will be in the seam allowance protruding at the beginning of the ring. Enter these same pins through the right side of the other end of the ring, making sure that the ring is not twisted. Use a pricking movement until you are able to find and push the pins through in the right place *(Figure 414)*. Push the layers against the pin heads with the pins being perpendicular to the seam line.

Pin the layers together to keep them from shifting whilst stitching the seam. I use three pins for this, placing them at right angles to the seam line.

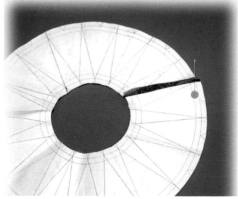

*Figure 414*

Remove the pins used for positioning and stitch the seam from edge to edge. Sitich very close but not on the paper *(Figure 415)*. Trim the seam allowance to a scant $1/4$" and press to one side. The outer ring is now complete .

*Figure 415*

## PIECING THE INNER RING

The inner ring is made in exactly the same way as the outer ring. Using one of the photocopies, cut out the inner ring section *(Figure 407, page 25)* and make this ring following the instructions for the outer ring. Both rings are now complete.

## APPLIQUEING THE CENTRE

There are many ways to appliqué the centre onto the ring. You may well have an appliqué technique that suits you and this is the method that you should use. Some of the patterns in the book have large centres which could be pieced into the ring but they were, in fact, all made with appliquéd centres. I actually enjoy appliquéing on the centres and for the most part it is the easiest way to do it. I have also seen it done very successfully using fancy machine stitches to appliqué the centre. You could also consider using the blind hem method to appliqué by machine or use a satin stitch. I will give hand appliqué methods which work well for me with this type of piecing.

## LARGE APPLIQUED CIRCLES

Use the centre section of the photocopy which was leftover from the outer ring. Trim it roughly $1/8$" larger than the dotted cutting line for the centre section *(Figure 409, page*

25). Place it on the square cut for the appliquéd centre. Sew exactly on the solid seam line using a long stitch - I use stitch setting 4 *(Left Figure 416)*. This line of stitching is purely a marker indicating the place where the edge will be turned under. If this is stitched in a contrasting thread it will be easier to see. Cut on outer dotted line. Tear the paper away, leaving the stitches intact. Do this with care as the stitches are large *(Right Figure 416)*.

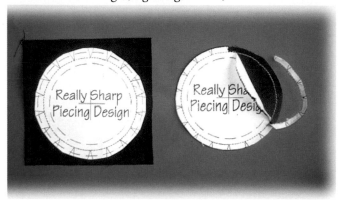

*Figure 416*

Thread a needle with contrasting thread and baste the edge under. Pleat in the fullness as you go. I've found that loading 6-8 stitches on the needle at one time is not only quicker but produces a smoother curve *(Left Figure 417)*. Press the circle flat and remove the long machine stitches which are on the fold line. Check that you don't have any notches around the curved edge. If you do find some, they can be pressed out using the tip of the iron to manipulate the seam allowance.

Lay the inner ring flat and place the centre onto it to check the size. Use a matching thread and sew the centre onto the ring. I've

*Figure 417*

found it helpful to line up the edge with about three points of the ring, then stitch a little way, line up another point, stitch a bit more, line up another point thus working my way around the circle *(Figure 418)*.

The stitch I use is a ladder stitch and makes the edge lie very flat. Ladder stitch is achieved by taking $1/16$" stitches from the background fabric and immediately the needle emerges take an equal stitch

*Figure 418*

in the fold line of the appliqué piece. To avoid a bulged out centre, be sure to work with the ring flat on a table.

Remove the basting stitches.

## SMALL APPLIQUED CIRCLES

The above method works well on most circles but for ones which are less than 2" I would suggest another approach. It is the method that uses a rigid template for the circle and gives a smoother edge on smaller circles. Glue a copy of the appliqué centre onto a piece of cardboard which is firm but not thick. Cut it out very carefully on the solid seam line. The fabric pieces for appliqué should be cut out on the cutting line. Machine baste using a long stitch around the fabric circle about $^1/_8$" in from the edge. Leave long threads at the beginning and end of this line of stitching. Place the template disc in the centre of the wrong side of the fabric. Gently pull the long threads to gather the edges and pull them in over the template. Knot the threads to secure it while you appliqué. Press before appliquéing and also check the size. I leave the template in position whilst appliquéing and remove it by snipping into the seam allowance slightly if necessary after it is in place. Attach it to the ring using the same methods as for the larger circles. This is the method I used when making the small blocks for Solstice, Columns and A Fishy Affair.

## CURVED SEAMS

Sewing curves is something many quilters view with trepidation. The very idea used to be enough to put me off even considering any design which involved curved seams. This continued until I changed my attitude. Now I see a curved seam as a line of stitching made up of many very small straight segments. These straight segments are the areas between the needle and the next pin. I use a lot of pins and the result is a kind of sewing dot-to-dot or in this case, pin-to-pin. This way I need only worry about a very small area at one time.

## THE OUTER CURVED SEAM

This method does not involve clipping the seam allowances at any time. Find and match one of the marks on the background fabric to one of the points on the outside edge of the outer ring, right sides together. If necessary, be sure the ring is orientated correctly within the background. With the paper on top, level the edges and insert a straight pin at right angles to the curved seam. Do not pin directly through the bulk of the point but about $^1/_8$" to one side of it. Skip the next mark and point.

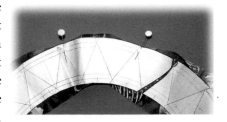

Match and pin the following point, again $^1/_8$" to one side. Now go back and pin the point which lies between the two pins. Pin $^1/_8$" on each side of this point. Pin the section between the points, placing the pins no more than about $^3/_4$" apart.

A lot of pins? Yes, but it works and makes sewing the curve trouble-free. If you are new to sewing curves, I suggest that you now stitch the pinned section before pinning any more. Continue to work with short segments, building up the length of them over a period. This is the method I used when I first started sewing curves and it certainly made things easier as well as building up my confidence.

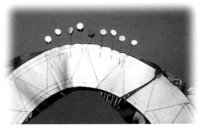

You will be stitching with a small stitch setting. Stitch, paper side up, on the solid seam line. Position the edge under the machine so that the first stitch falls after the first pin. Lower the needle through the seam line. Now adjust the fabrics to avoid sewing those annoying tucks into the background fabric. Use your thumbs to feel underneath and sort out just the area between the needle and the next pin you will come to when stitching. Make sure that just that little area is flat. It may seem awkward at first but will soon become second nature. Stitch the pinned segment, removing each pin just before the needle reaches it. Each time you stop to remove a pin, use your thumbs underneath to sort out the fabrics between it and the next pin along.

You may well get a tuck in your first attempts but very quickly this will improve and you will begin to feel confident. Then the tucks that do occur will be quite rare. This is when you should start pinning and sewing a slightly longer segment, building up the length of the segment point by point as your confidence grows. Soon, the number of pins you have available to use will be the only limiting factor with regards to the length of the curve you sew at one go.

There is no need to back stitch these segments. Pin another section and sew in the same way, overlapping the stitching by just about $^1/_4$". Do not start and stop on the pieced points because of the bulk of the seams. Continue working your way around the circle until it is complete. As you go, check the points on the right side to be sure they are sharp. If you find one you don't like the look of, carefully undo about a $^1/_2$" on each side of the point. Lift or lower the point to correctly position it. Pin and stitch, overlapping the stitches by about $^1/_4$" at the beginning and at the end.

After sewing in the entire ring, lay the block flat right

side up and finger press the seam. Turn the block over and remove the paper foundation, taking care not to stretch the inside edge of the ring.

## THE INNER CURVED SEAM

The pinning and stitching methods are the same as those used for the outer ring. In order to get sharp points on the outer ring, it is very important to make sure the edges are absolutely level especially where there is a point on the outer ring.

The only real difference between sewing the inner and outer curves is the positioning markers. For the outer ring, you marked the background fabric. On the inner ring, the positioning marks are automatically made for you. Look at the paper seam allowance on the outer edge of the inner ring. Between the pieced points of this ring, you will see little "v" shapes. These v-shapes are the cut-off tips of the pieced points in the outer ring. Therefore, they will serve as the perfect positioning markers for sewing in the inner ring. Match a v-shape to a point in the outer ring, right sides together *(Figure 419)*. Pin and sew this curve in the same way as for the outer curve to complete the block. Finger press and then press with the iron, working with the right side uppermost. Remove all paper foundations.

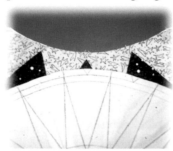

*Figure 419*

## 1-RING CIRCULAR PIECING

One-Ring Circular Piecing is easy - just follow the 2-Ring Circular Piecing instructions for making up the units of the block. The only real difference being that you are using only one ring. Take care to use the correct cutting line when making the freezer paper template for cutting the hole from the background fabric. Remember that the template is for the hole which is cut out and discarded. It must be $1/4$" smaller than the finished size of the circle that you want to sew into the background. This is to allow for seam allowances on the background fabric around the edge of the circle. For instance, if you wanted to make a 1-ring block using only the inner ring of the Really Sharp Piecing design *(Figure 420)*, the cutting line for the freezer paper template would be the fourth dotted line in

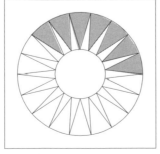

*Figure 420*

from the outside edge of the design as printed in *Figure 421*. After piecing the ring I still appliqué the centre onto the ring before piecing it into the background. Once the centre is attached, sew the ring into the prepared background square following instructions for "Curved Seams", on page 33. After completing the block, press from the top and then remove the foundation paper.

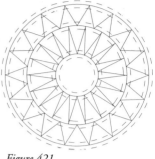

*Figure 421*

## CURVED UNIT PIECING

Curved units are sections of curved foundation piecing which run from one edge of a block to another edge of the block. Very often these units are quarter circles such as those used in the blocks for Sunny Side Up and Autumn Forest.

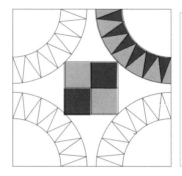

In the large block for Solstice, there are two curved units. The smaller unit is a quarter circle and the larger one is an oddly shaped unit. They are both pieced in the same way because although they are different shapes they are both curved units which run from one edge of the block to another edge of the same block.

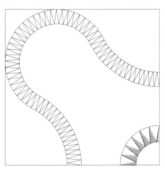

Using a photocopy, cut out the pattern for the curved unit roughly $3/8$" larger than the solid seam line on all sides. This will be about $1/8$" *outside* of the dotted cutting line. If necessary refer to the section in "Understanding The Full-Size Pattern" which deals with curved unit blocks on page 24.

Piece the curved unit as described in "Piecing The Outer Ring", on page 30. The piecing of a curved unit is exactly the same as for piecing a full ring except for the fact that it does not actually form a full ring. In most cases there will be no need to roll up the pattern but with longer units it be easier if you work using the scroll method. After completing the unit trim the curved edges exactly on the dotted cutting line. Trim the straight edges as described in "Trimming", on page 36.

The pinning and sewing of the curves is the same as described in "Curved Seams", on page 33. For me, sewing full circle curves is always easier than sewing a curved unit to the other pieces of a block. I have found that problems can occur at the beginning and the end of the curved seam, sometimes causing the edges of the block to be uneven. To get around these problems, simply do away with the beginning and ending by sewing the first and last $^1/_2$" of the curved seam. Line up the edges of the first $^1/_2$" of the seam, right sides together, and pin. Stitch, with the paper uppermost, on the seam line for $^1/_2$" and remove from the machine. In *Figure 422*, you can see the curved unit with the piece which will be added to it to complete the block. In *Figure 423*, the first $^1/_2$" of the seam has been stitched. Although it was stitched from the other side, this side is shown for clarity and the contrasting thread ends have been left in place to indicate the beginning and end of the stitching.

| Figure 422 | Figure 423 |

Bring the other ends of the curved seam together, edges even, and pin. Stitch the last $^1/_2$" of the curved seam. In *Figure 424*, this $^1/_2$" has been sewn and the seam pinned, ready for stitching the rest of the curved seam. The seams would be stitched from the other side with the foundation paper on top. The seam will be sewn in the same way as a circular seam, pressing the seam allowance away from the pieced unit. Sew any remaining curved seams in the block in this way.

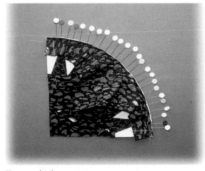

Figure 424

Remove the foundation papers from the block, leaving a couple intact on any outside edge of the block *(Figure 425)*.

*Figure 425*

These will not only help to stabilise the block but will also be helpful in getting sharp points when sewing the block together with other sections of the quilt. The only reason I suggest removing any of the pieces now is to avoid having to remove them from the entire quilt all at one time. I always leave foundations in place on raw edges. If a piece is completely enclosed with finished seams, the foundation paper can be removed.

## NON-CIRCULAR BLOCKS

Although these are blocks which have straight edges, they are still made using the ring-piecing techniques. There will be no curved seams and fewer seam allowances shown on the pattern. Although some of the smaller blocks may have the seam allowance marked on the outside straight edges, the larger ones will not. This is because you will use the rotary cutter to add the $^1/_4$" seam allowance when you trim the finished block as detailed in "Trimming", on page 36. The smaller blocks which have their seam allowances included are also trimmed with the rotary cutter. The reason for printing the seam allowances on these small blocks is to indicate clearly that they are full-size patterns.

Using one of the photocopies, cut out the block roughly $^3/_8$" larger than the solid seam line on all sides. This can be done with the rotary cutter and ruler. Using scissors, cut through the ring exactly on a solid seam line for one of the points. Do not cut this line on a corner or an angled edge of the block but rather on a straight edge as this will help to keep the points which go into the corners or angles really sharp. This is important because the corner is often where the eye first lands when looking at a finished block of this type.

Cut out the centre, this time cutting about $^1/_8$" inside of the dotted cutting line. Follow the instructions for "Piecing The Outer Ring", on page 30, but do not trim the block. Appliqué the centre, following instructions for "Appliquéing The Centre", on page 32.

Foundation piecing can be used to add more pieces on to these blocks because they have straight edges. In the block for Spring Greens on page 88, the C pieces for the corners are added in this way. To add these pieces, lay the triangle cut for the C piece, right side up on the sewing machine extension table. Position the block over it with the paper uppermost. A scant $^1/_4$" seam allowance should be on the triangle-side of the seam line with most of the C piece lying under the pieced ring *(Figure 426)*.

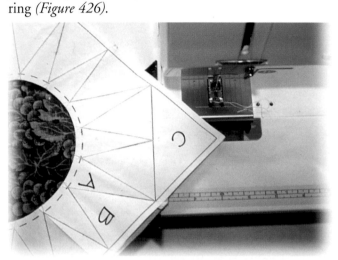

*Figure 426*

Sew this seam in the same way as the seams of the ring were sewn. Press the piece open to form a corner on the pieced ring. Sew on the other corners to complete the block.

## STRAIGHT UNIT PIECING

The patterns for straight units are all printed without seam allowances. These units will be trimmed as detailed in "Trimming", to include $^1/_4$" seam allowance after the unit is completely pieced. Cut out the pattern roughly $^3/_8$" larger than the solid seam line on all sides. This can be done using the rotary cutter and ruler.

For long units you will have to glue photocopies together to form the correct pattern. Always overlap by a square or triangle in order to ensure a straight edge for the length of the unit. At times it will be necessary to cut off part of a photocopied pattern in order to get the correct pattern configuration. When this happens, be sure to cut roughly $^3/_8$" beyond the final solid seam line required for the pattern. On long units, it is extremely important to check and double check that you have glued your foundation pattern together correctly.

The piecing of a straight unit, long or short, is the same as used in "Piecing The Outer Ring", on page 30, except for the fact you are making a straight unit and do not cut into or join into a ring. Remember to piece long units in a scroll fashion although this will not be necessary for short units.

## TRIMMING

Almost all of the straight edged patterns in the book do not have the seam allowance included on the pattern. Use the rotary cutter and ruler to trim and very accurately add the $^1/_4$" seam allowance at the same time. The method is the same whether it is a block or a straight unit and whether or not seam allowances were printed on the pattern. Add the seam allowance to each side as you cut by positioning the $^1/_4$" line of the ruler on the solid seam line of the block or unit. Always check the placement of the ruler several times, up and down the seam, before cutting. Check this placement again after you have applied pressure on the ruler as the paper makes the ruler more likely to slip. When trimming a unit which is longer than the ruler, simply position the ruler on a segment of the unit - about 15" at a time - and trim. Move the unit along on the cutting board and position the ruler and trim another section of the unit. To ensure a straight edge on long units, be sure to overlap by placing the ruler on part of the previously cut section.

This brief chapter brings good news to those of you who love to make miniature quilts. The techniques presented in this book work exceeding well when used in miniature. In fact, the very first block I made using these methods could almost be called a miniature as it was the 6³/₄" sashing block from Solstice. You don't have to be a maker of miniature quilts to find good uses for very small, sharply pieced blocks. In Columns, on page 52, the miniature block plays a leading role in the overall design of the full-size quilt. The 4" sashing blocks in A Fishy Affair, on page 38, don't have such a starring role but nonetheless add a definite something to the design of the quilt.

Making complicated blocks like these would be very difficult by traditional means, especially when working on a small scale, but they become an absolute piece of cake when made with foundation piecing. The methods are exactly the same, the only difference being that the pieces are smaller. With very small pieced circles, you may find it easier to appliqué the pieced section onto the background square, although it is surprising just how small of a circle can be sewn by machine. To make any of the blocks in this book smaller, simply use a photocopy machine to reduce them to the desired size. Seam allowances for the foundation piecing should be trimmed to ¹/₈" as you sew.

The block you see below is a full-size reproduction of a very small quilt made by Cathy Corbishley Michel, measuring just 5⁵/₈" x 5¹/₂". Cathy has a very demanding career which, according to her, "interferes with her quilting life". Knowing this, it was with great reservations that I asked if she would like to make a miniature using the design for the block in her quilt, Sunflowers, on page 92. A few days later she telephoned me, thrilled with the ease and speed of making the block in miniature.

## A FISHY AFFAIR

*Quiltmaker:* Barbara Barber, Hampshire, England, 1996
*Quilt size:* 86" x 86"

This was the first quilt I made using blocks from my Really Sharp Piecing workshops.
The two fish print fabrics used for the background of the blocks were chosen in the first of those workshops
which was at Country Threads in Bath. Those "fishy" fabrics determined the rest of the colours in the quilt.
Although very bright, it's certainly a quilt we enjoy sleeping under.

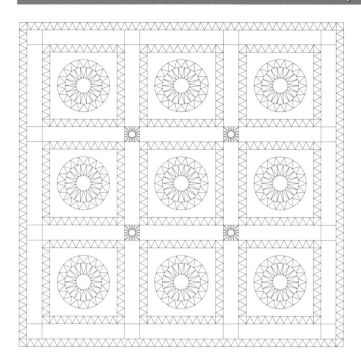

## CUTTING

*From the black "fish" fabric, cut:*
4 squares, each $18^{1}/_{2}$" x $18^{1}/_{2}$", for the background of 4 of the blocks.

*From the turquoise "fish" fabric, cut:*
5 squares, each $18^{1}/_{2}$" x $18^{1}/_{2}$", for the background of 5 of the blocks.

*From EACH of the 9 different prints in green, orange and turquoise, cut:*
2 strips, each $2^{1}/_{2}$" x 44". From these strips cut 18 pieces, each $2^{1}/_{2}$" x $3^{1}/_{4}$", for the D pieces in each of the blocks.
4 strips, each $3^{1}/_{2}$" x 44". From these strips cut 64 pieces, each $3^{1}/_{2}$" x $2^{3}/_{8}$", for the E pieces in each of the blocks and the triangles on the outer edges of the border.

*From EACH of the 9 different yellow prints, cut:*
1 strip, 4" x 44". From this strip cut 18 pieces, each 4" x $2^{1}/_{8}$", for the B pieces in each of the blocks.
1 strip, $3^{1}/_{4}$" x 44". From this strip cut 18 pieces, each $3^{1}/_{4}$" x $2^{1}/_{8}$", for the C pieces in each of the blocks.
4 strips, each $3^{1}/_{2}$" x 44". From these strips cut 59 pieces, each $3^{1}/_{2}$" x $2^{3}/_{8}$", for the F pieces in each of the blocks and the inner triangles in the border.

*From EACH of the 9 different multi-coloured prints in red, black and blue, cut:*
2 strips, each $1^{1}/_{4}$" x 44". From these strips cut 18 pieces, each $1^{1}/_{4}$" x 4", for the A pieces in each of the blocks.
1 square, $4^{3}/_{4}$" x $4^{3}/_{4}$", for the appliquéd centre in each of the blocks.

## MATERIALS:

*44"-wide fabric*

$1^{1}/_{4}$ yds. black "fish" fabric for the background of 4 of the blocks

$1^{5}/_{8}$ yds. turquoise "fish" fabric for the background of 5 of the blocks

$5/_{8}$ yd. EACH of 9 different prints in green, orange and turquoise for the blocks and borders

$3/_{4}$ yd. EACH of 9 different yellow prints for the blocks, borders and the 4 small sashing blocks

$3/_{8}$ yd. EACH of 9 different multi-coloured prints in red, black and blue for the blocks, the sashing squares and the 4 small sashing blocks

2 yds. stripe fabric for the sashing

$5/_{8}$ yd. black print for the binding

$7^{7}/_{8}$ yds. for the backing

90" x 90" piece of wadding

15" x 15" square freezer paper

## PHOTOCOPIES

19 copies of Really Sharp Piecing Design *(found on sheets in back pocket of book)*

5 copies of A Fishy Affair Sashing Block *(page 41)*

18 copies of A Fishy Affair Section 1 *(found on sheets in back pocket of book)*

18 copies of A Fishy Affair Section 2 *(found on sheets in back pocket of book)*

Copies of A Fishy Affair Section 1 & 2 as required to make up border foundations

## CUTTING continued

*For the sashing squares, cut:*

12 squares, each 4½" x 4½", from the 9 different multi-coloured prints in red, black and blue.

*For each of the 4 sashing blocks, cut:*

1 strip, 3" x 44", from one of the multi-coloured prints in red, black and blue. From this strip cut 16 pieces, each 3" x ¾", for the G pieces.

1 square, 2½" x 2½", from the same multi-coloured print for the appliquéd centre.

1 strip, 3" x 44", from one of the yellow prints. From this strip cut 16 pieces, each 3" x 1¾", for the H pieces.

*From the stripe fabric, cut:*

24 strips, each 4½" x 22½", for the sashing.

## PIECING

1. Make 9 Really Sharp Piecing blocks using the 18½" x 18½" squares for the background of the blocks and the pieces cut for the A, B, C and D pieces. Use the 4¾" x 4¾" squares for the appliquéd centres. Refer to "2-Ring Circular Piecing" on page 29.

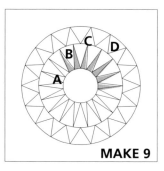

**MAKE 9**

2. Using the pieces cut for the E and F pieces, make up 18 each of A Fishy Affair Section 1 and A Fishy Affair Section 2. Refer to "Straight Unit Piecing" on page 36. Trim each of the units, following the instructions for "Trimming" on page 36.

**MAKE 18 OF EACH**

3. Sew one of the shorter units to both the top and the bottom of each of the blocks made in step 1. Add a longer pieced unit to each side of each of the blocks. Press the seam allowances toward the block.

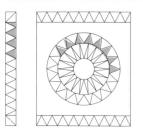 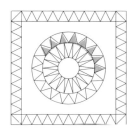

**MAKE 9**

4. Make 4 small sashing blocks using copies of the Sashing Block. Refer to "Non-Circular Blocks" on page 35. Use the pieces cut for the G and H pieces and the 2½" x 2½" square for the appliquéd centre. Trim the outer edges

of the blocks, referring to "Trimming" on page 36.

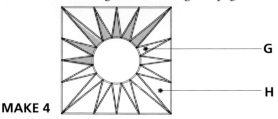

**MAKE 4**

5. Arrange the blocks with the sashing strips, the sashing squares and sashing blocks. Sew into rows, continually pressing the seams toward the sashing strips.

Sew the rows together to form the centre of the quilt. Press the seams to one side. Remove the foundation papers from the sashing square blocks.

6. Prepare the paper foundations for the pieced border by gluing together copies of A Fishy Affair Sections 1 & 2. To ensure accuracy, overlap the units by one whole triangle when gluing the copies together. For more information about gluing photocopied design together, see page 23. When preparing foundation papers for a long string of piecing, I find it very helpful to number the individual units. By writing directly on the foundations, I am certain to end up with the correct size strip which has the correct number of pieces.

**MAKE 2 OF EACH**

Use the pieces cut from the 9 different prints in green, orange and turquoise at random for the outer triangles in the border sections and the pieces cut from the different yellows for the inner triangles in the border. Piece the border, referring to "Straight Unit Piecing" on page 36. Trim the borders as described in "Trimming" on page 36.

7. Add one of the shorter border sections to the top and one to the bottom of the quilt. Find and match the centres before pinning and then stitching. Stitch with the pieced borders uppermost, using the seamline on the paper as a guide. Press the seam allowances toward the sashing.

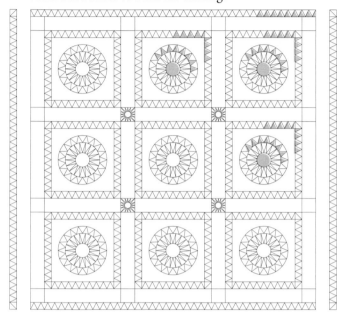

Sew the longer border sections to each side of the quilt as above.

8. If necessary mark the top with quilting designs of your choice. A Fishy Affair did not require marking. All of the seams were quilted in-the-ditch and the sashing was quilted between each stripe on the fabric. The background of the blocks was free-motion quilted in a wave formation to carry out the theme of the fish fabrics.

9. Just before layering the top with the wadding and backing, carefully remove the paper foundations from the pieced borders. Leaving the papers intact on the outer edges until just before layering the quilt will prevent the pieced section from stretching out of shape. Layer the top, wadding and backing. Pin or baste and then quilt as desired. Bind the edges and add a label.

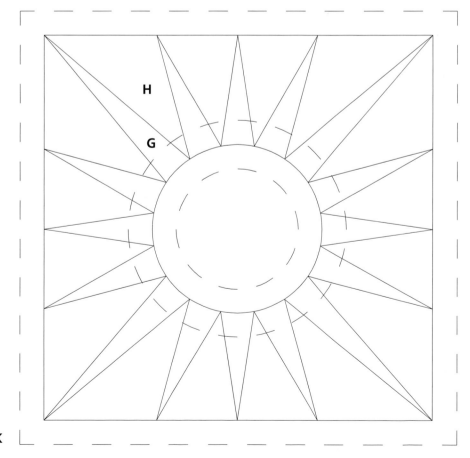

**TEMPLATE**

**SASHING BLOCK**

## AUTUMN FOREST

*Quiltmaker:* Shirley Shotton, Oxford, England, 1997
*Quilt size:* $73^{1}/_{2}$" x $73^{1}/_{2}$"

What a wonderful collection of leafy fabrics there are in this quilt!
Shirley used 64 different leaf fabrics and a great assortment of plaids
for a stunning combination with all the plain fabrics.

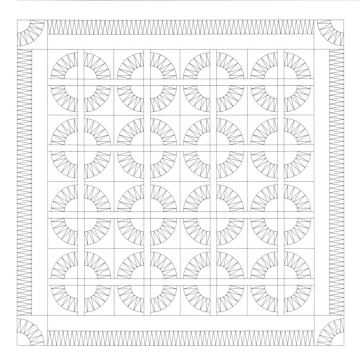

## CUTTING

*From the assorted "leaf" fabrics, cut:*
64 D pieces for the blocks. Use photocopies as described in "Photocopied Templates", on page 26, to cut out the shapes.

*From the plain fabrics, for each block, cut:*
1 C piece (a total of 68 required for all the blocks). Use photocopies as described in "Photocopied Templates", on page 26, to cut out the shapes.
7 rectangles, each 4" x 2", for the B pieces in the blocks (a total of 476 required for all the blocks).

*From the assorted plaids, cut:*
6 rectangles, each 4" x 1$^1/_4$", for the A pieces in each block ( a total of 408 required for all the blocks).
9 strips, each 4$^1/_4$" x 44". From these strips cut 240 rectangles, each 4$^1/_4$" x 1$^1/_2$", for the pieced outer border.
1 strip, 2" x 44". From this strip cut 16 squares, each 2" x 2", for the sashing squares.

*From the green print, cut:*
NOTE: Cut the border strips first from the lengthwise grain of the fabric.
4 strips, each 4" x 60$^1/_2$", for the inner border.
4 D pieces for the corner blocks. Use photocopies as described in "Photocopied Templates", on page 26, to cut out the shapes.
16 strips, each 7$^1/_4$" x 2", for sashing strips.
24 strips, each 14" x 2", for sashing strips.
244 rectangles, each 4$^1/_4$" x 1$^1/_2$", for the pieced outer border. Cut 4$^1/_4$" strips across the remaining width of the fabric and then cut into the rectangles.

## MATERIALS:
*44"-wide fabric*

2$^3/_4$ yds. total assorted "leaf" fabrics for the blocks

3$^1/_4$ yds. total plain fabrics in a range of colours for the blocks

3$^1/_4$ yds. total assorted plaid fabrics for the blocks, the outer border, the sashing squares and the binding

3$^1/_2$ yds. green print for the four corner blocks, the sashing, the inner border and the outer border

4$^1/_2$ yds. for backing

78" x 78" piece of wadding

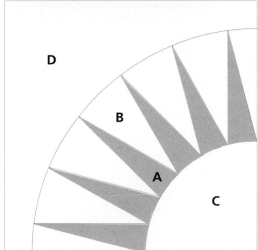

## PHOTOCOPIES

68 copies of Autumn Forest Block *(page 67)*

Extra copies of Autumn Forest as needed to make templates for the C and D pieces.

Copies as required of Autumn Forest Border Section *(found on sheets in back pocket of book)*

## PIECING

1. Make 68 Autumn Forest blocks. Refer to "Curved-Unit Piecing" on page 34. Use the plaids cut for the A pieces and the plain fabrics cut for the B and C pieces in all of the blocks. Use the "leaf" fabrics cut for the D pieces in 64 of the blocks. In the 4 corner blocks, use the green print for the D pieces.

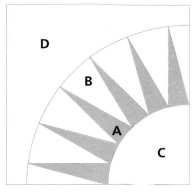

2. Sew 60 of the blocks into pairs. Do not use the 4 corner blocks. Press all the seams in one direction.

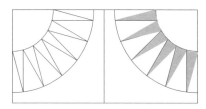

Sew 18 of the pairs together to make 9 units made up of 4 blocks each. Press the seams to one side.

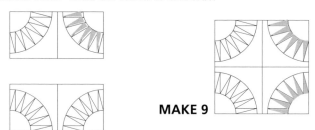

MAKE 9

3. Arrange these units with the sashing strips and the sashing squares. Sew the units together to form rows, continually press the seams toward the sashing strips.

Sew the rows together to form the centre of the quilt, pressing seams to one side. Remove any foundation papers remaining in the blocks.

4. Prepare the paper foundations for the pieced border by gluing together copies of Autumn Forest Border Section. To ensure accuracy, overlap the units by one whole triangle when gluing the copies together. For more information about gluing photocopied designs together, see page 23. When preparing foundation papers for a long string of piecing, I find it very helpful to number the individual units. By writing directly on the foundations, I am certain to end up with the correct size strip which has the correct number of pieces. Make one border for each side of the quilt.

There are 60 whole triangles along the outer edge of the border. Use the plaid pieces for the triangles on the outer edge and the green print pieces for the triangles on the inner edge. Piece the borders, referring to "Straight Unit Piecing" on page 36. Trim the borders as described in "Trimming" on page 36.

5. Add a 4" x 60$\frac{1}{2}$" green print border strip to each pieced border unit. Find and match the centres before pinning and then stitching. Stitch with the pieced borders uppermost, using the seamline on the paper as a guide. Press the seam allowances away from the pieced unit.

6. Add a pieced border unit to the top and the bottom of the quilt. Find and match up the centres before pinning and then stitching. Press the seam towards the border.

7. Sew a corner block to each end of the 2 remaining border units, pressing the seams away from the blocks. Sew one of

these units to each side of the quilt. Find and match up the centres before pinning and then stitching. Press the seam towards the border.

8. Mark the top with quilting designs of your choice. All seams of Autumn Forest were quilted in-the-ditch before being quilted as shown.

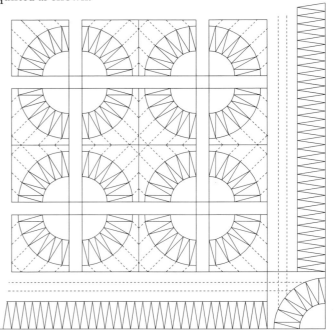

9. Just before layering the top with the wadding and backing, carefully remove the paper foundations from the pieced borders. Leaving the papers intact on the outer edges until just before layering the quilt will prevent the pieced section from stretching out of shape. Layer the top, wadding and backing. Pin or baste and then quilt as desired. Bind the edges and add a label.

# AZDAZ

*Quiltmaker:* Lois Andrews, Surrey, England, 1997
*Quilt size:* 78¹/₂" x 78¹/₂"

Feathered star designs always look so very complicated and difficult and although this is not a quilt for a beginner,
it is easier to make using the foundation methods than one might at first suppose.
The circular design in the centre of the block adds to it's impact.
Lois' inspiration for colours came from her daughter's school Aztec Project.
With regards to the close quilting, Lois adds, "Long-sighted ladies of a certain age will appreciate
the difficulties and I took up wearing glasses during the project!".

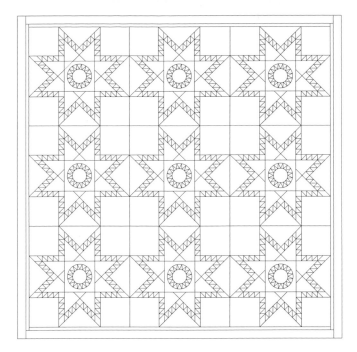

## CUTTING

*From the yellow print, cut:*

*NOTE: Cut the border strips first from the lengthwise grain of the fabric.*

2 strips each, $1^1/_4$" x $73^1/_2$", for the inner border.

2 strips each, $1^1/_4$" x 75", for the inner border.

18 strips, each $2^1/_2$" by the width of the fabric. From these strips cut 288 squares, each $2^1/_2$" x $2^1/_2$". Cut each square once diagonally to give 576 triangles for the E pieces in the blocks.

9 squares, each $11^3/_8$" x $11^3/_8$". Cut each square twice diagonally to give 36 triangles for the H pieces in the blocks.

36 squares, each $7^5/_8$" x $7^5/_8$", for the K pieces in the blocks.

*From the gold print, cut:*

6 strips each 2" x 44". From these strips cut 144 pieces, each 2" x $1^1/_2$", for the B pieces in the blocks.

*From the turquoise, cut:*

5 strips, each 2" x 44". From these strips cut 144 pieces, each 2" x $1^1/_4$", for the A pieces in the blocks.

1 strip, $4^1/_2$" x 44". From this strip cut 9 squares, each

## MATERIALS:

*44"-wide fabric*

4 yds. yellow print for the blocks and the inner border.

$^3/_8$ yd. gold print for the centre ring in the blocks.

$1^1/_8$ yds. turquoise for the blocks.

$1^1/_2$ yds. pink print for the blocks.

4 yds. green print for the blocks, the outer border and the binding.

$4^7/_8$ yds. for the backing.

83" x 83" piece of wadding.

7" x 7" square of freezer paper

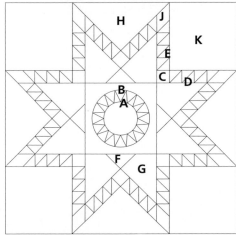

## PHOTOCOPIES

19 copies of Azdaz Circle Design *(page 51)*

36 copies of Azdaz Unit L *(page 71)*

36 copies of Azdaz Unit M *(page 71)*

36 copies of Azdaz Unit N *(page 50)*

36 copies of Azdaz Unit P *(page 50)*

Copies of Azdaz G as required *(page 51)*

## CUTTING continued

$4^1/_2$" x $4^1/_2$", for the appliquéd centres in the blocks.
5 strips, each $4^1/_2$" x 44". From these strips cut 72 rectangles, each $4^1/_2$" x $2^1/_2$", for the J pieces in the blocks.

*From the pink print, cut:*
4 strips, each 2" x 44". From these strips cut 72 squares, each 2" x 2", for the C pieces in the blocks.
14 strips, each $2^1/_2$" x 44". From these strips cut 216 squares, each $2^1/_2$" x $2^1/_2$". Cut each square once diagonally to give 432 triangles for the D pieces in the blocks.

1 strip, $4^3/_8$" x 44". From this strip cut 9 squares, each $4^3/_8$" x $4^3/_8$". Cut each square twice diagonally to give 36 triangles for the F pieces in the blocks.

*From the green print, cut:*
*NOTE: Cut the border strips first from the lengthwise grain of the fabric.*
2 strips, each $2^1/_2$" x 75", for the outer borders.
2 strips, each $2^1/_2$" x 79", for the outer borders.
9 squares, each 8" x 8", for the centre square in the blocks.
5 strips, each $8^1/_2$" by the width of the fabric. Refer to "Photocopied Templates", on page 26. Using copies of the Azdaz G Template as described, cut 72 pieces for the G pieces in the blocks.

## PIECING

1. Make the blocks for the central square in the feathered star. Refer to "1-Ring Piecing" on page 34. Use the 8" x 8" green print squares, the turquoise A pieces, the gold print B pieces and the $4^1/_2$" x $4^1/_2$" turquoise squares for the appliquéd centres. Use the photocopies of Azdaz Circle Design.

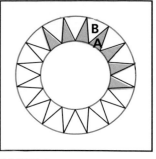

**MAKE 9**

2. Piece the units for the feathers of the star. Refer to "Straight Unit Piecing" on page 36. Use the pieces cut for the C, D, E and J pieces in the block to make up 36 of each of the Azdaz Units L, M, N and P. Trim the units as described in "Trimming" on page 36.

**MAKE 36 OF EACH UNIT**

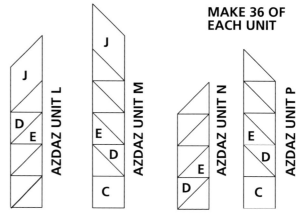

3. To make the construction easier and to avoid set-in seams, partial seams are used in the sewing of the feathered star blocks. A partial seam is one that is not sewn right the way through but only sewn between certain indicated points. Add an Azdaz Unit N to each H piece; use a partial seam, sewing from point X to point Y only. Sew with the paper foundation on top, using the line as a stitching line to assure sharp points on the feathers. Press the seam towards the H piece.
Add Azdaz Unit P. Using a partial seam, with the paper foundation on top, sew from point X to point Y only. Press the seam towards the H piece.

4. Add a G piece to each unit. Stitch with the foundation on top and press the seam towards the G piece.

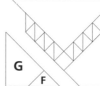

Sew an F piece to a G piece. Stitch with the foundation on top and press the seam towards the G piece. Add this to the unit, pressing the seam towards F/G piece.

5. Add the Azdaz Unit L to a square K piece, stitching with the foundation paper uppermost. Press the seam allowance towards the K piece.

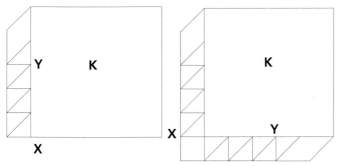

Add the Azdaz Unit M, sewing with the foundation paper uppermost. Press the seam towards the K piece.

6. Arrange the pieced units in rows as shown. Sew the units together, pinning carefully and stitching with the foundation paper on top when possible. When sewing the K and H Units together in Rows 1 and 3, stitch from the inner corner outwards with the foundation paper uppermost. Then finish sewing the partial seams from points Y to the edge of the block. Press the seam away from the feathered units. Sew Rows 1 and 3 to Row 2 in the same way, pressing seams toward one side.

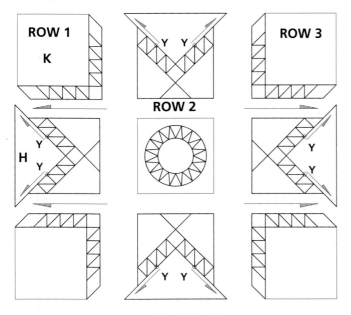

**MAKE 9 BLOCKS**

Remove all the paper foundations from all the blocks.

7. Sew the blocks together to form rows, pressing seams to one side. Sew the rows together to form the centre of the quilt. Press seams to one side. *See top of next column.*

8. Add the $1^{1}/_{4}$" x $73^{1}/_{2}$" inner border strips to the top on bottom of the quilt. Find and match the centres before pinning and stitching. Add the $1^{1}/_{4}$" x 75" inner border strips to the

sides of the quilt in the same manner.

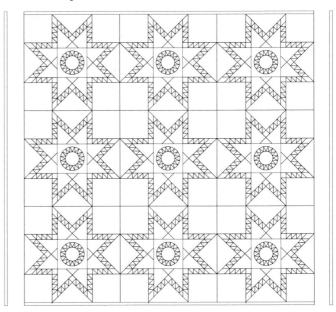

9. The outer borders are sewn on in the same way using the ones cut $2^{1}/_{2}$" x 75" for the top and bottom and the ones cut $2^{1}/_{2}$" x 79" for the sides. *See over page.*

10. If necessary, mark the top with quilting patterns of your choice. Azdaz did not require marking. All of the seams were quilted in-the-ditch before all of the larger areas were quilted with random machine stippling.

11. Layer the top, wadding and backing. Pin or baste and then quilt as desired. Bind the edges and add a label.

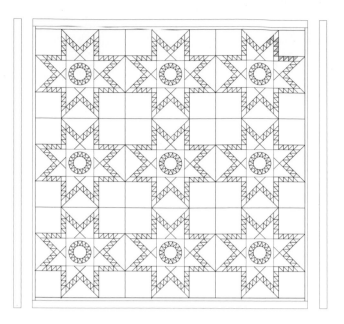

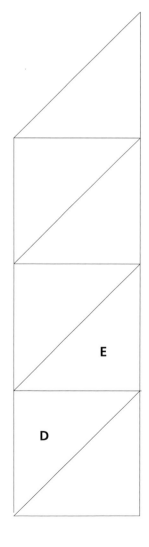

**E**

**D**

**TEMPLATE**

**AZDAZ
UNITS**

**AZDAZ UNIT N**

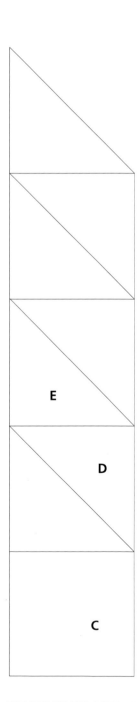

**E**

**D**

**C**

**AZDAZ UNIT P**

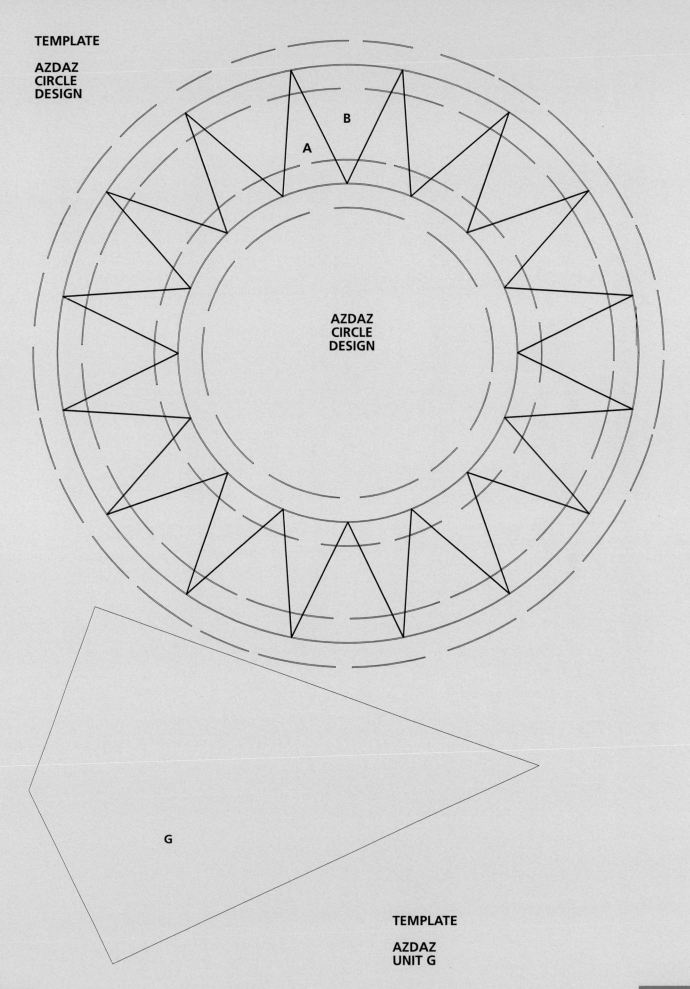

TEMPLATE

AZDAZ
CIRCLE
DESIGN

B

A

AZDAZ
CIRCLE
DESIGN

G

TEMPLATE

AZDAZ
UNIT G

# COLUMNS

*Quiltmaker:* Barbara Barber, Hampshire, England, 1997
*Quilt size:* 90" x 90"

When I designed this quilt, the sashing reminded me of architectural columns.
Scrap quilts are often stunning with their wide array of fabrics but sometimes
the simplest combination of several fabrics can be just as effective.
This quilt needs a lot of quilting to make it work and the quilting designs are included with the pattern.

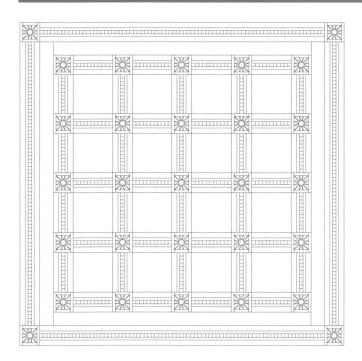

## CUTTING

*From the red, cut:*

*NOTE: Cut the long border strips first from the lengthwise grain of the fabric.*

8 strips, each $1^1/4$" x $79^1/2$", for the borders.

80 strips, each $1^1/4$" x $11^1/2$", for the sashing.

58 strips, each $1^1/4$" x $4^1/2$", for the sashing block frame.

58 strips, each $1^1/4$" x 6", for the sashing block frame.

29 squares, each $2^1/4$" x $2^1/4$", for the appliquéd centres of the sashing blocks.

7 strips, each $3^1/2$" x 44". From these strips cut 348 pieces, each $3^1/2$" x $^3/4$", for the A pieces in the sashing blocks.

25 strips, each $1^1/2$" x 44", for the checkered centre strip in the sashing and the border.

*From the yellow, cut:*

17 strips, each $3^1/4$" x 44". From these strips cut 348 pieces, each $3^1/4$" x 2", for the B pieces in the sashing blocks.

28 strips, each $1^1/2$" x 44", for the checkered centre strip in the sashing and the border.

*From the cream, cut:*

*NOTE: Cut the long border strips first from the lengthwise grain of the fabric.*

2 strips, each $4^1/4$" x 72", for the inner border.

2 strips, each $4^1/4$" x $79^1/2$", for the inner border.

8 strips, each 2" x $79^1/2$", for the outer border.

80 strips, each 2" x $11^1/2$", for the sashing.

16 squares, each $11^1/2$" x $11^1/2$", for the plain blocks.

## MATERIALS:

*44"-wide fabric*

$3^1/2$ yds. red

$2^7/8$ yds. yellow

$5^1/2$ yds. cream

$8^1/4$ yds. for the backing

94" x 94" piece of wadding

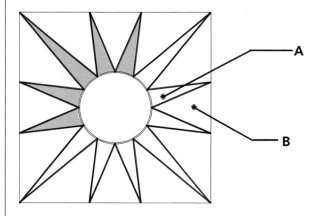

## PHOTOCOPIES

31 copies of Columns Sashing Block *(page 83)*

1 copy of Columns Quilting Design *(found on sheets in back pocket of book)*

1 copy of Columns Border Quilting Pattern *(found on sheets in back pocket of book)*

## PIECING

1. Refer to "Non-circular Blocks" on page 35. Make 29 blocks using photocopies of the Columns Sashing Block. Use the pieces cut for the A and B pieces and the squares cut for the appliquéd centres. Trim all of the blocks as described in "Trimming" on page 36.

2. Sew a $1^1/_2$" x $4^1/_2$" red strip onto the top and bottom of each block, pressing the seam away from the block. Stitch these seams with the paper foundation on top, using the line as a guide. Add a $1^1/_2$" x 6" red strip to each side of the blocks to form the block frame. Press seams away from the block. Remove all foundation papers from the blocks.

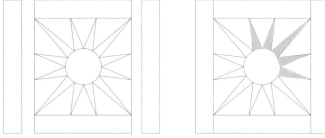

**MAKE 29**

3. The checkered centre strip in the sashing is made using strip piecing techniques. Sew together $1^1/_2$" wide red and yellow strips into sets before sewing sets together to eventually make a panel of 11 strips, starting and ending with a yellow strip. Press each seam closed, as sewn, before opening out the strip and pressing the seam towards the red strip. This will help to keep the panel of strips straight and keep them from twisting. Press each seam in this way before sewing the next seam. From this panel of 11 strips, cut off $1^1/_2$" wide segments to form the centre of the sashing. You will need 40 of these segments for the sashing.

4. Sew a red strip, $1^1/_4$" x $11^1/_2$", to each side of each of the segments prepared in Step 3, pressing the seam allowances toward

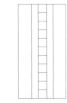

**MAKE 40**

the red strip. Add a cream strip, 2" x $11^1/_2$", to each side of these units, pressing the seam allowances toward the red strip.

5. Lay out the sashing units with the sashing blocks and the $11^1/_2$" x $11^1/_2$" cream squares to form rows. Sew the sashing blocks to sashing units, pressing the seams toward the sashing blocks. Sew the sashing units to the cream squares, pressing the seam allowances toward the cream square. Pin carefully and then stitch the rows together to form the centre of the quilt.

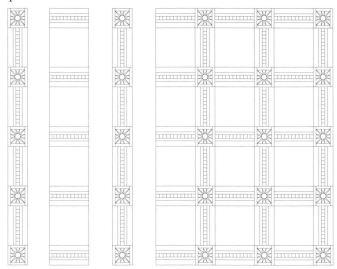

6. Add the $4^1/_4$" x 72" cream strips to the top and bottom of the quilt. Find and match the centres and pin before stitching. Press the seams away from the cream strip. Sew the $4^1/_4$" x $79^1/_2$" cream strips to each side in the same way.

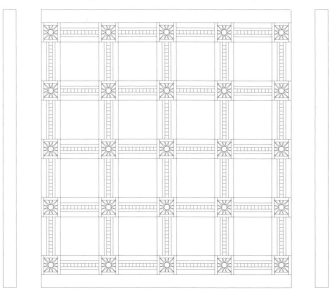

7. Make the checkered centre for the outer border in the same way you made the checkered centre for the sashing units. This time use 10 strips, each $1^1/_2$" wide, to make the panel of strips. Use 5 yellow and 5 red strips alternately. The 10 strip panel will start with a yellow strip and end with a red strip. Cut $1^1/_2$" wide segments from the panel of strips. You will need 32 of these segments to make the border.

Each side of the border has 40 yellow and 39 red squares,

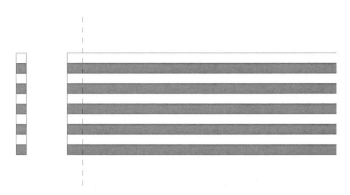

making a total of 79 squares per side. For each side, sew together 8 of the checkered segments into a long string, keeping to the yellow, red, yellow, red sequence. Use your seam ripper to remove one red square from the end of this long string. This will result in the string of squares starting and ending with a yellow square.

**MAKE 4**

Use the $1^1/_4$" x $79^1/_2$" red strips and the 2" x $79^1/_2$" cream strips to make up the borders in the same way as the sashing units were made in Step 4.

8. Sew a border unit to the top and the bottom of the quilt. Find and match the centres, pin and the stitch. Press the seam allowances away from the outer border. Sew a pieced block to each end of the remaining 2 border units, pressing the seam towards the block. Add these border units to the quilt in the same way as before. This time press the seam towards the outer border unit.

10. Layer the quilt top with the wadding and backing. Pin or baste and then quilt as desired. When binding the quilt, change the colour of the binding to match the edge of the quilt. Do this as you come to each corner, and use a straight seam to join the new colour of binding in keeping with the edge of the quilt. Add a label to complete the quilt.

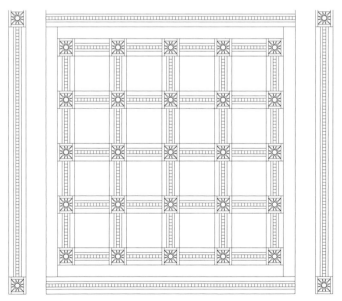

9. To quilt your quilt as shown, mark the top using a copy of Columns Quilting Design and Columns Border Quilting Pattern. This can be done easily with a light box. If the fabric is very light coloured as in Columns, you may be able to simply trace the design through the fabric without the aid of a light box. This will be made easier if you darken the lines on the copy of the quilting design with a permanent

## GEOFF & THE BEARS

*Quiltmaker:* Barbara Barber, Hampshire, England, 1997
*Quilt size:* 74" x 74"

This quilt holds the memories of many happy workshops.
The name itself is the result of a weekend teaching at The Cotton Patch in Birmingham.
Nowhere could I find just the right fabric for the sashing. During the course of the weekend, in desperation
I threw the blocks at Geoff Sewell, one of the owners, but I didn't really think he'd have any luck either.
His intelligent interest in colour and texture certainly surprised me.
I was even more surprised when later on he came back with the perfect fabrics for the block frames and the sashing.

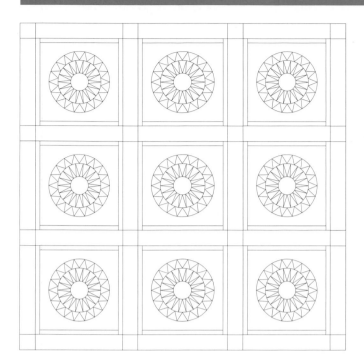

## MATERIALS:

*44"-wide fabric*

$2^3/_4$ yds. printed "bear" fabric for background of blocks

$1^1/_8$ yds. green print for block frame

$1/_4$ yd. black print for setting squares

$1^1/_2$ yds. black stripe for sashing

$1^7/_8$ yds. assorted yellow prints for blocks

$7/_8$ yd. assorted red prints for blocks

$1^1/_4$ yds. assorted blue prints for blocks

$1/_2$ yd. black print for binding

$4^5/_8$ yds. for standard backing *(For optional pieced backing, see page 60)*

78" x 78" piece of wadding

15" x 15" piece of freezer paper

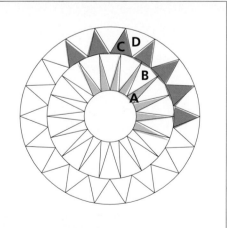

## CUTTING

*From the "bear" fabric for the background of blocks, cut:*
9 squares, each $18^1/_2$" x $18^1/_2$"

*From the green print for the block frame, cut:*
1 piece, $18^1/_2$" x 44". From this piece cut 18 strips, each $18^1/_2$" x $1^1/_2$"
1 piece, $20^1/_2$" x 44". From this piece 18 strips, each $20^1/_2$" x $1^1/_2$"

*From the black print for the setting squares, cut:*
2 strips, each 4" x 44". From these strips cut 16 squares, each 4" x 4"

*From the black stripe for the sashing, cut:*
12 strips, each 4" x 44". From these strips cut 24 rectangles, each 4" x $20^1/_2$"

*For each block, cut:*
2 red strips, each $1^1/_4$" x 44". From these strips cut 18 rectangles, each $1^1/_4$" x 4" for the A pieces
1 red square, $4^3/_4$" x $4^3/_4$", for the appliquéd centre
1 yellow strip, 4" x 44". From this strip cut 18 rectangles, each 4" x $2^1/_8$", for the B pieces
1 yellow strip, $3^1/_4$" x 44". From this strip cut 18 rectangles, each $3^1/_4$" x $2^1/_8$", for the C pieces
2 blue strips, each $2^1/_2$" x 44". From these strips cut 18 rectangles, $2^1/_2$" x $3^1/_4$", for the D piece

## PHOTOCOPIES

19 copies of Really Sharp Piecing Design *(found on sheets in back pocket of book)*

## PIECING

1. Following the instructions for "2-Ring Circular Piecing" on page 29, make 9 blocks. Use the 18¹/₂" x 18¹/₂" bear fabric and the 18 rectangles cut for each of the A, B, C and D pieces. Use the 4³/₄" x 4³/₄" red square for the appliquéd centre. Remove the paper foundations from the blocks.

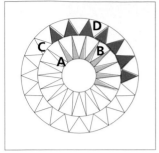

**MAKE 4**

2. Using the green block frame strips, sew a 1¹/₂" x 18¹/₂" strip to the top and bottom of each block.

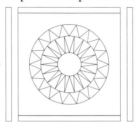 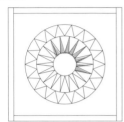

Sew a 1¹/₂" x 20¹/₂" strip to each side of the block. Press the seam allowances toward the green.

3. Arrange the blocks with the sashing strips and setting squares as shown. Sew into rows, pressing the seams toward the sashing strips. Sew the rows together.

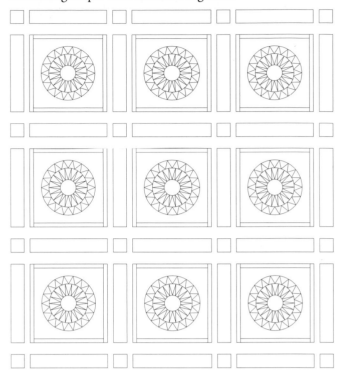

4. If necessary, mark the quilt top with your chosen design. The quilting in Geoff & The Bears did not require marking. All seams were quilted in-the-ditch. A line of stitching was quilted between each stripe in the sashing. The background of the blocks, the setting squares and the appliquéd centres were all quilted with a large, open stipple by machine.

5. Layer the quilt top with the wadding and backing. Pin or baste and then quilt as desired. Bind the edges and add a label.

**TEMPLATE**   **SOLSTICE SASHING BLOCK**

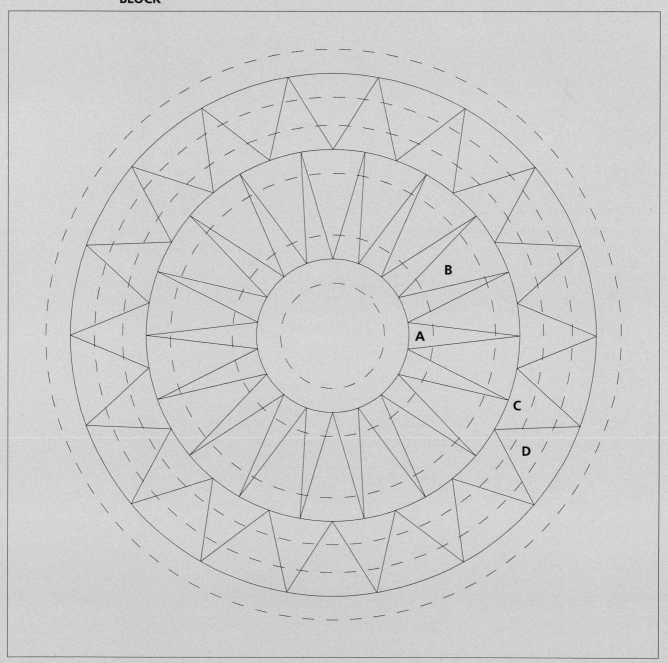

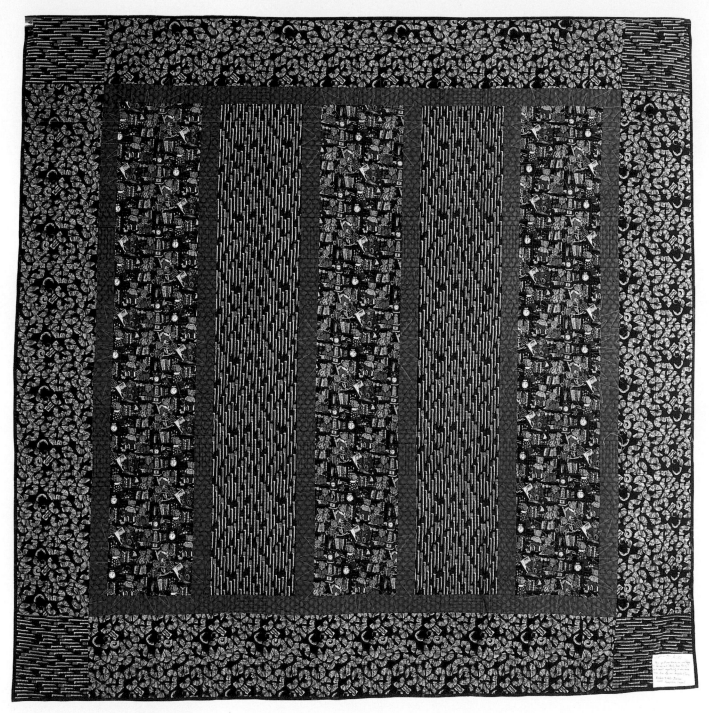

## GEOFF & THE BEARS - PIECED BACK

*Quiltmaker:* Barbara Barber, Hampshire, England, 1997
*Quilt backing size:* 77" x 77"

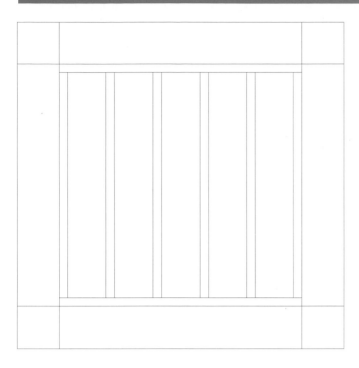

## CUTTING

All pieces are cut from the lengthwise grain of the fabric.

*From the "bear" print, cut:*
3 strips, each , $9^1/_2$" x $53^1/_2$"

*From the black stripe , cut:*
2 strips, each $9^1/_2$" x $53^1/_2$"
4 squares, each $10^1/_2$" x $10^1/_2$"

*From the green print, cut:*
6 strips, each $2^1/_2$" x $53^1/_2$"
2 strips, each $2^1/_2$" x $57^1/_2$"

*From the black print, cut:*
4 strips each $10^1/_2$" x $57^1/_2$"

## MATERIALS:

*44"-wide fabric*

$1^5/_8$ yds. "bear" print

$1^5/_8$ yds. black stripe

$1^3/_4$ yds. green print

$1^3/_4$ yds. black print

*NOTE: If you are using the same fabrics for the pieced backing as you did in the quilt top, you can save fabric. Re-calculate the top and backing together according to your fabric choices.*

## PIECING

1. Referring to the diagram and the photograph, piece the centre section.

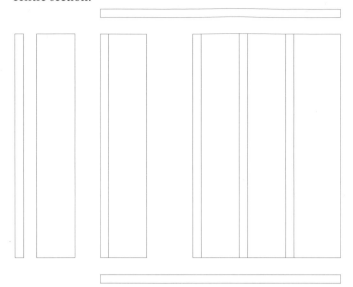

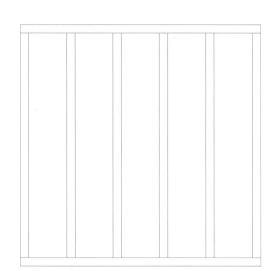

Press the seams to one side.

2. Sew a $10^{1}/_{2}$" x $10^{1}/_{2}$" square onto both ends of 2 of the $10^{1}/_{2}$" x $57^{1}/_{2}$" black print strips.

Press the seam allowances toward the long strips.

3. Stitch the remaining seams according to the diagram. Press seam allowances toward the long outer strips of black print fabric.

4. Layer the backing with the prepared quilt top and wadding. Take extra care to match the centres of the top and backing before pinning or basting. Quilt as desired. Label and bind to complete.

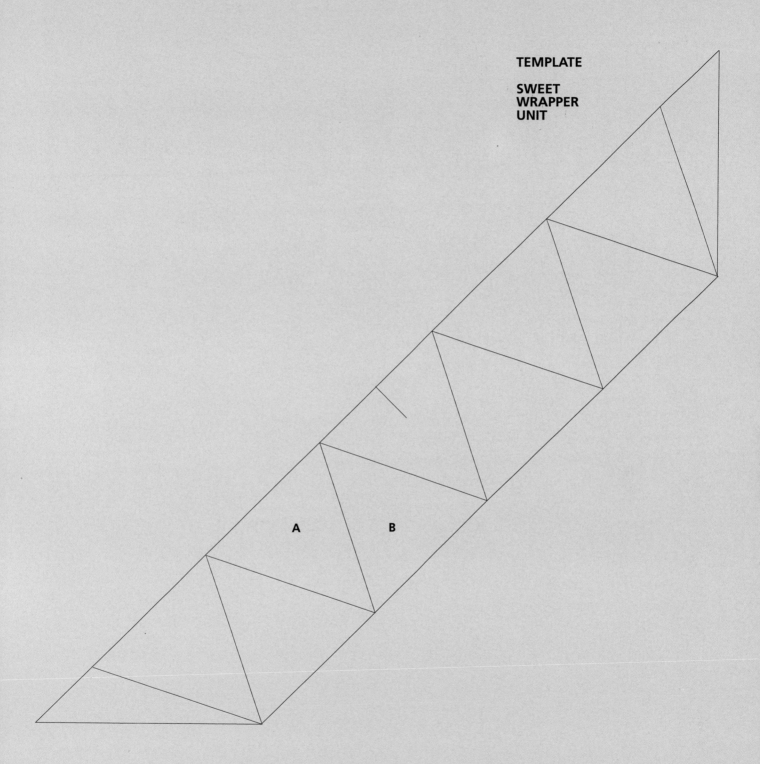

**TEMPLATE**

**SWEET
WRAPPER
UNIT**

A    B

# HEXSTAR

*Quiltmaker:* Julie Standen, Bristol, England, 1997
*Quilt size:* 69$\frac{1}{4}$" x 75"

Julie made Hexstar amidst total chaos. Her house was practically being rebuilt around her as she worked.
The builders seemed to lack an appreciation for quiltmaking
but Julie found that working on this quilt during a difficult time helped to keep her sane.
The off-cuts from piecing this quilt were quite large so Julie used them to make Leftover Geese at the same time.

## MATERIALS:

*44"-wide fabric*

$5^1/_4$ yds. cream print for blocks and binding

$1^1/_2$ yds. dark print for setting triangles

$2^7/_8$ yds. total assorted purple, pink and turquoise prints for blocks

$4^3/_8$ yds. for backing

74" x 79" piece wadding

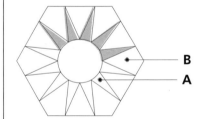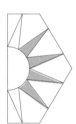

B
A

## CUTTING:

*From the cream print, cut:*

36 strips, each $4^1/_2$" x 44". From these strips cut 246 rectangles, each $4^1/_2$" x 6" for the B pieces

*From the dark print, cut:*

6 strips, each $8^1/_2$" x 44". Refer to "Photocopied Templates", page 26. Using the copies as described, cut 36 setting triangles and 8 half setting triangles.

*From the purple, pink and turquoise prints, for each whole block, cut:*

2 strips, each 2" x 44". From these strips cut 12 rectangles each, 2" x 6", for the A pieces

1 square, $6^1/_2$" x $6^1/_2$" for the appliquéd centre

*From the purple, pink and turquoise prints, for each half block, cut:*

1 strip, 2" x 44". From this strip cut 6 rectangles, each 2" x 6", for the A pieces

1 rectangle, $6^1/_2$" x 5" for the appliquéd centre

## PHOTOCOPIES

34 copies of Hexstar Block *(found on sheets in back pocket of book)*

12 copies of Hexstar Half-Block *(The solid line which runs through the centre of the full Hexstar Block is the seam line for the Half-Blocks. Use copies of one half of the Hexstar Block found on sheets in the back pocket of the book)*

Copies of Hexstar Setting Triangle and Hexstar Half Setting Triangle as required *(for the Hexstar Half Setting Triangle use half of the Hexstar Setting Triangle found on sheets in back pocket of book)*

## PIECING

1. Referring to "Non-Circular Blocks" on page 35, make 17 Hexstar blocks. Use the 2" x 6" rectangles for the A pieces, the $4^1/2$" x 6" rectangles for the B pieces and the $6^1/2$" x

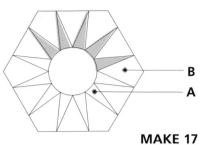
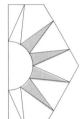

**B**

**A**

**MAKE 17**

$6^1/2$" square for the appliquéd centre. Trim the outer edges of the blocks, referring to "Trimming" on page 36.

2. Make 6 half Hexstar blocks, following the instructions for "Non-Circular Blocks" on page 35. Use the A and B pieces and the $6^1/2$" x 5" rectangle for the appliquéd centre. Trim the outer edges of the blocks as in Step 1.

**MAKE 6**

3. Use the dark print setting triangles and the half setting triangles to make up units and then rows. Continually press the seam allowances toward the setting triangles. Sew the rows together, pressing seams to one side.

4. Mark the quilt top with quilting designs of your choice. The stars in Hexstar were quilted in-the-ditch before the rest of it was quilted as shown.

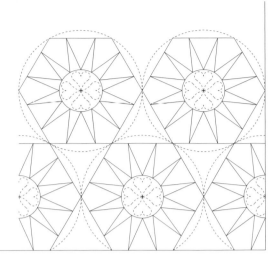

5. Layer the top, wadding and backing. Pin or baste and then quilt. Bind the edges and then add a label.

**AUTUMN
FOREST
BLOCK**

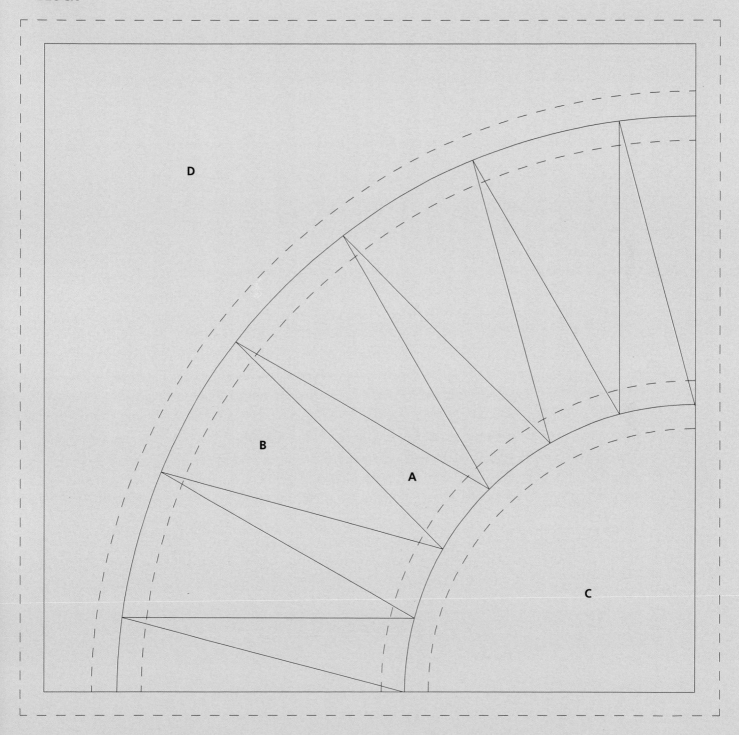

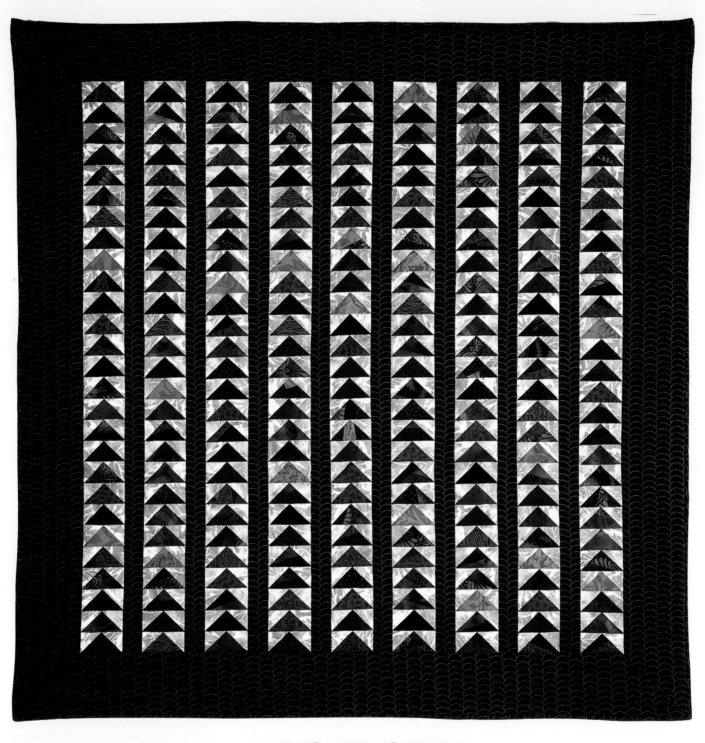

## LEFTOVER GEESE

*Quiltmaker:* Julie Standen, Bristol, England, 1997
*Quilt size:* 48" x 49$^{1}/_{2}$"

Julie pieced Hexstar, on page 64, and this quilt simultaneously. As the off-cuts from the first piled up,
she used them to piece the geese strips. At times, she sewed small bits together before using them to piece the geese.
This allowed her to use even the tiniest bits and it also looks very effective.
Best of all, upon completion, Julie had two lovely quilts.

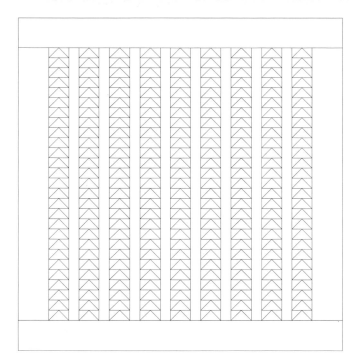

## CUTTING

*From the assorted purple, pink and turquoise prints, cut:*
11 strips, each $3^1/2$"x 44". From these strips cut 122 squares, each $3^1/2$" x $3^1/2$". Cut each square once diagonally for 243 triangles needed for the geese

*From the cream print, cut:*
16 strips, each $2^1/2$"x 44". From these strips cut 243 squares, each $2^1/2$" x $2^1/2$". Cut each square once diagonally for 486 triangles for the background of the geese

*From the lengthwise grain of the purple print, cut:*
8 strips, each 2" x 41" for the sashing
2 strips, each 5" x 41" for the border
2 strips, each 5" x $48^1/2$" for the border

## MATERIALS

$1^1/4$ yds. total assorted purples, pinks and turquoise prints for geese

$1^1/4$ yds. cream print for background of geese

$1^1/2$ yds. purple print for sashing, border and binding

3 yds. for backing

54" x 54" piece of wadding

*NOTE: If this quilt is made from the off-cuts from the blocks in Hexstar, on page 64, there will be sufficient to piece all of the geese strips. If you are not using those off-cuts, follow the fabric requirements listed.*

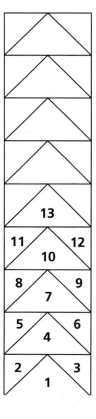

## PHOTOCOPIES

Copies as required of Leftover Geese Unit

## PIECING

1. Prepare the paper foundations for the strips of pieced geese by gluing together copies of Leftover Geese Unit. To ensure accuracy, overlap the units by one whole rectangle when gluing the copies together. For more information about gluing photocopied designs together see page 23. When preparing foundation papers for a long string of piecing, I find it very helpful to number the individual units on the foundation. By writing directly on the foundation, I am certain to end up with the correct size strip which has the correct number of pieces. Glue the photocopies together to make foundation units as shown. There are 27 geese in each strip. The piecing sequence is shown numbered on page 69.

2. Piece the 9 geese strips using the assorted purple, pink and turquoise print triangles for the geese and the cream print for the background. Refer to "Straight Unit Piecing" on page 36. Trim the units, referring to "Trimming" on page 36.

3. Make up the centre of the quilt by sewing the geese strips to the 2" x 41" sashing strips. Find and match the centre points first and then pin at frequent intervals before stitching. Sew with the paper on top, stitching on the line. This will give perfect points to the edge of the geese.

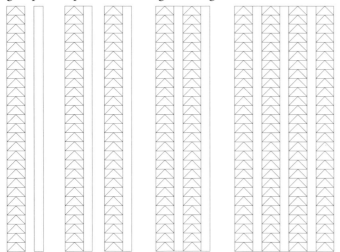

Press the seam allowances toward the sashing strips.

4. Add a 5" x 41" border strip to each side, pinning and stitching as in Step 3. Press the seam allowances towards the borders.

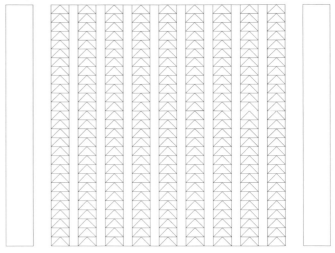

5. Sew the 5" x 48$^1/_2$" border strips to the top and bottom. Match centres, pin well and sew with paper side up. Press the seam allowances toward the borders.

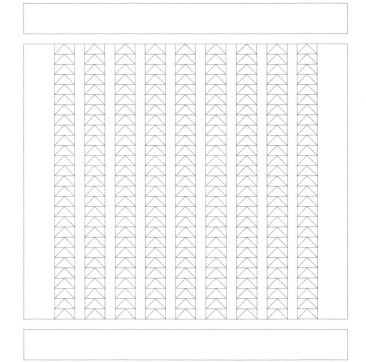

Remove all the paper foundations.

6. If necessary mark the quilt top with the quilting design of your choice. Leftover Geese did not require marking. All seams were quilted in-the-ditch. Two straight lines of quilting were stitched in the border, spaced 1$^1/_2$" apart.

7. Layer the quilt top with the wadding and backing. Pin or baste and then quilt as desired. Bind the edges and add a label.

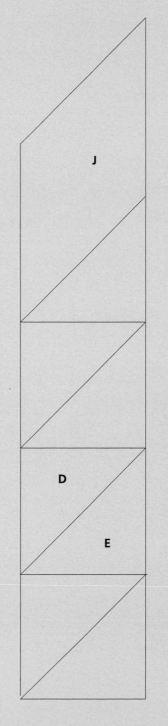

**AZDAZ UNIT L**

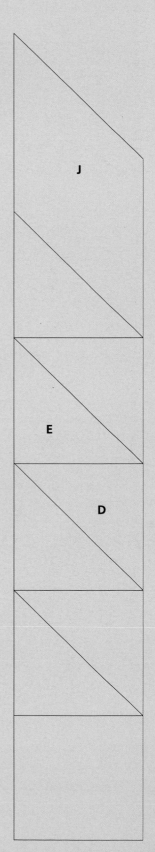

**AZDAZ UNIT M**

**TEMPLATE**

**AZDAZ
UNITS**

# MERIDIAN

*Quiltmaker:* Shelagh Jarvis, London, England, 1997
*Quilt size:* 80¹/₂" x 80¹/₂"

The design for the block in this quilt was inspired by the logo for our
television channel in the south which is called Meridian.
During the making of this quilt, Shelagh had several bouts of serious ill health and therefore
I feel very privileged to be able to include it.
She is well on the road to recovery and her grandson will be delighted with the quilt.

# *MERIDIAN*

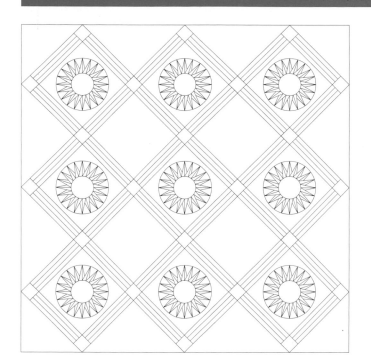

## MATERIALS:

*44"-wide fabric*

2³/₄ yds. navy print for the plain blocks and the setting triangles

1 yd. navy for sashing strips and the binding

2⁵/₈ yds. yellow

2⁵/₈ yds. orange print

1¹/₂ yds. blue print

1 yd. green print

5 yds. for backing

85" x 85" piece of wadding

15" x 15" piece of freezer paper

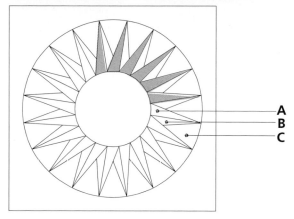

## CUTTING

*From the navy print, cut:*

4 squares, each 15¹/₂" x 15¹/₂", for the plain blocks.

4 squares, each 18⁷/₈" x 18⁷/₈". Cut each square once diagonally for 8 setting triangles.

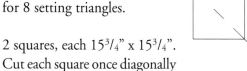

2 squares, each 15³/₄" x 15³/₄". Cut each square once diagonally for 4 corner triangles.

*From the navy, cut:*

1 piece, 15¹/₂" x 44". From this piece cut 24 strips, each 15¹/₂" x 1¹/₂", for sashing strips.

*From the yellow, cut:*

1 strip, 3¹/₂" x 44". From this strip cut 12 squares, each 3¹/₂" x 3¹/₂", for sashing squares.

1 piece, 15¹/₂" x 44". From this piece cut 20 strips, each 15¹/₂" x 1¹/₂", for sashing strips.

3 strips, each 4³/₄" x 44". From these strips cut 100 pieces, each 4³/₄" x 1¹/₄", for the B pieces in 5 of the blocks.

5 strips, each 3³/₄" x 44". From these strips cut 80 pieces, each 3³/₄" x 2¹/₂", for the C pieces in 4 of the blocks.

4 squares, each 15¹/₂" x 15¹/₂", for the background for 4 of the blocks.

## PHOTOCOPIES

19 copies of Meridian Design *(found on sheets in back pocket of book)*

## CUTTING continued

*From the orange print, cut:*

8 squares, each $3^1/_2$" x $3^1/_2$", for sashing squares.

1 piece, $15^1/_2$" x 44". From this piece cut 20 strips, each $15^1/_2$" x $1^1/_2$", for sashing strips.

1 strip, 5" x 44". From this strip cut 20 pieces, each 5" x $1^1/_4$", for the A pieces in 1 of the blocks.

3 strips, each $4^3/_4$" x 44". From these strips cut 80 pieces, each $4^3/_4$" x $1^1/_4$", for the B pieces in 4 of the blocks.

5 strips, each $3^3/_4$" x 44". From these strips cut 80 pieces, each $3^3/_4$" x $2^1/_2$", for the C pieces in 4 of the blocks.

4 squares, each $15^1/_2$" x $15^1/_2$", for the background for 4 of the blocks.

1 square, $6^1/_2$" x $6^1/_2$", for the appliquéd centre in 1 of the blocks.

*From the blue print, cut:*

1 piece, $15^1/_2$" x 44". From this piece cut 24 strips, each $15^1/_2$" x $1^1/_2$", for sashing strips.

3 strips, each 5" x 44". From these strips cut 80 pieces, each 5" x $1^1/_4$", for the A pieces in 4 of the blocks.

2 strips, each $2^1/_2$" x 44". From these strips cut 20 pieces, each $2^1/_2$" x $3^3/_4$", for the C pieces in 1 of the blocks.

1 square, $15^1/_2$" x $15^1/_2$", for the background for 1 of the blocks.

4 squares, each $6^1/_2$" x $6^1/_2$", for the appliquéd centre in 4 of the blocks.

*From the green print, cut:*

4 squares, each $3^1/_2$" x $3^1/_2$", for sashing squares.

1 piece, $15^1/_2$" x 44". From this piece cut 20 strips, each $15^1/_2$" x $1^1/_2$", for sashing strips.

3 strips, each 5" x 44". From these strips cut 80 pieces, each 5" x $1^1/_4$", for the A pieces in 4 of the blocks.

1 square, $6^1/_2$" x $6^1/_2$", for the appliquéd centre in 1 of the blocks.

## PIECING

*NOTE: This quilt is made up of 9 blocks. The blocks are all pieced from the same pattern. The effect is achieved by altering the colours within the blocks. This quilt requires 3 different colour arrangements in the blocks. To make the quilt as shown, use the following colour arrangements for the blocks.*

4 blocks using the orange print for the background squares and the C pieces, the green print for the A pieces and the appliquéd centre and the yellow print for the B pieces.

4 blocks using the yellow print for the background squares and the C pieces, the blue print for the A pieces and the appliquéd centre and the orange print for the B pieces.

1 block using the blue print for the background squares and the C pieces, the orange print for the A pieces and the appliquéd centre and the blue print for the C pieces.

1. Referring to "1-Ring Circular Piecing" on page 34, make 9 blocks. Use the $15^1/_2$" x $15^1/_2$" background squares, the $6^1/_2$" x $6^1/_2$" squares for the appliquéd centre, and the pieces cut for the A, B and C pieces. For colour placement, refer to the photograph and the note above. Most Ring Piecing can be done by adding pieces around the circle, starting in either direction. In this block, however, it can only be pieced in one direction. Make the cut through the ring in the position indicated and start piecing in the direction of the arrow. The numbers show the order in which the pieces are added. Carry on around the circle in this way.

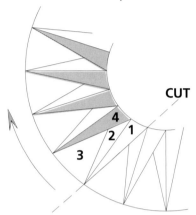

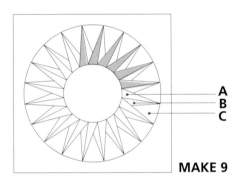

MAKE 9

2. Sew the $15^1/_2$" x $1^1/_2$" sashing strips together into sets of three, referring to the photograph for colour placement. Make 36 units made up from 3 strips each.

3. Arrange the blocks with the sashing units, the sashing squares and the $15^1/_2$" x $15^1/_2$" navy print squares. Sew into rows, pressing the seams away from the sashing units.

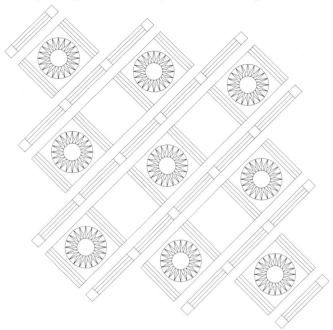

Add the navy print setting triangles, pressing seams away from the sashing units.

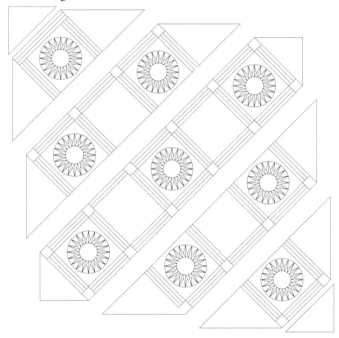

Sew the rows together, pressing seams to one side.

4. If necessary, mark the quilt top with designs of your choice. The quilting used for Meridian did not require any marking. All of the seams were quilted in-the-ditch. The larger areas of the quilt were then stippled by machine.

5. Layer the quilt top with the wadding and backing; pin or baste and then quilt as desired. Bind the edges and add a label.

# ROLL 'EM, ROLL 'EM, ROLL 'EM

*Quiltmaker:* Myra Ibbetson, Dorchester, England, 1996
*Quilt size:* 69" x 94$\frac{1}{4}$"

When I designed this quilt, it gave me the impression of wagon wheels.
In view of what she named her quilt, I think Myra must have thought so, too.
For the background of the blocks, Myra chose a fabric printed with an old-fashioned circus design.
This choice of fabric carries the theme throughout the quilt. Myra obviously enjoyed making this quilt because upon
completion she varied the design and made another which is shown on page 20.

## MATERIALS:

*44"-wide fabric*

1 yd. red for the sashing

2$^{1}/_{2}$ yds. blue print for the inner border, the setting squares and the binding

4$^{1}/_{2}$ yds. cream print for the background of the blocks and the outer border

1 yd. total assorted red prints for the A pieces

1$^{1}/_{4}$ yds. yellow print for the B pieces

$^{7}/_{8}$ yd. yellow print for the C pieces

1 yd. total assorted blue prints for the D pieces

5$^{3}/_{4}$ yds. for the backing

73" x 99" piece of wadding

12" x 24" piece of freezer paper

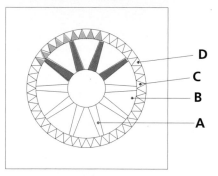

## CUTTING

*From the red, cut:*

2 pieces, each 15$^{1}/_{2}$" x 44". From these pieces cut 24 strips, each 15$^{1}/_{2}$" x 3$^{1}/_{2}$", for the sashing.

*From the blue print, cut:*

2 strips, each 3$^{1}/_{2}$" x 51$^{1}/_{2}$", for the inner border.

2 strips, each 3$^{1}/_{2}$" x 82$^{3}/_{4}$", for the inner border.

7 squares, each 3$^{1}/_{2}$" x 3$^{1}/_{2}$", for the setting squares.

3 squares, each 4$^{1}/_{4}$" x 4$^{1}/_{4}$". Cut each square twice diagonally to give the 12 setting triangles.

*From the cream print, cut:*

NOTE: *Cut the long border strips first.*

2 strips, each 6$^{1}/_{2}$" x 57$^{1}/_{2}$", for the outer border.

2 strips, each 6$^{1}/_{2}$" x 93$^{3}/_{4}$", for the outer border.

8 squares, each 15$^{1}/_{2}$" x 15$^{1}/_{2}$", for the background of the whole blocks.

3 squares, each 15$^{7}/_{8}$" x 15$^{7}/_{8}$". Cut each square once diagonally for the background of the half blocks.

## PHOTOCOPIES

17 copies of Roll'em Design *(found on sheets in back pocket of book)*

13 copies of Roll'em Half-Block Design *(the solid line which which runs through the centre of the full Roll'em Design is the seam line for the Half-Blocks. Use copies of one half of the Roll'em Design found on sheets in back pocket of book)*

9 copies of Roll'em Quarter-Block Design *(page 95)*

## CUTTING continued

1 square, $16^1/_4$" x $16^1/_4$". Cut this square twice diagonally for the background of the quarter blocks.

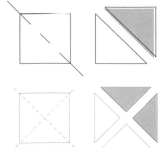

*From the yellow print for the B pieces, cut:*
10 strips, each $3^3/_4$" x 44". From these strips cut 128 pieces, each $3^3/_4$" x 3".

*From the yellow print for the C pieces, cut:*
23 strips, each $1^1/_4$" x 44". From these strips cut 480 pieces, each $1^1/_4$" x 2".

*For each of the whole blocks, cut:*
1 red strip, $1^1/_4$" x 44". From this strip cut 10 pieces, each $1^1/_4$" x 4", for the A pieces.
1 red square, $4^1/_2$" x $4^1/_2$", for the appliquéd centre.
2 blue strips, $1^1/_4$" x 44". From these strips cut 40 pieces, each $1^1/_4$" x 2", for the D pieces.

*For each of the half blocks, cut:*
1 red strip, $1^1/_4$" x 44". From this strip cut 5 pieces, each $1^1/_4$" x 4", for the A pieces.
1 red square, $4^1/_2$" x $4^1/_2$", for the appliquéd centre.
1 blue strip, $1^1/_4$" x 44". From this strip cut 21 pieces, each $1^1/_4$" x 2", for the D pieces.

*For each of the quarter blocks, cut:*
2 red pieces, each $1^1/_4$" x 4", for the A pieces.
1 red square, $4^1/_2$" x $4^1/_2$", for the appliquéd centre.
1 blue strip, $1^1/_4$" x 44". From this strip cut 11 pieces, each $1^1/_4$" x 2", for the D pieces.

## PIECING

1. Referring to the instructions for "2-Ring Circular Piecing" on page 29, make the whole blocks. Use the pieces cut for the A, B, C and D pieces, the appliquéd centre and the background squares. Take extra care when positioning the pieced rings into the background square to make sure all the spokes are correctly orientated.

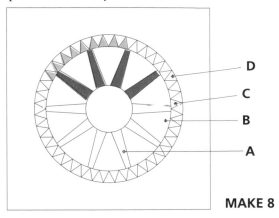

**MAKE 8**

Make the half blocks in the same way. The order in which the half blocks are put together is the same as for the whole blocks. Use the pieces cut for the A, B, C and D pieces, the appliquéd centre and the large background triangles. When preparing your photocopies, remember to add $1/_4$" seam allowance to the straight edge where you cut the design in half. This applies to all photocopies used for half blocks including those for the freezer paper template and the appliquéd centres. You can do this with your rotary cutter and ruler.

**MAKE 6**

Using the same methods, make the quarter blocks, following the instructions in "Curved Unit Piecing", on page 34. The order in which the quarter blocks are put together is the same as for the whole blocks. Use the pieces cut for the A, B, C and D pieces, the appliquéd centre and the smaller background triangles.

**MAKE 4**

2. Arrange the blocks with the sashing strips, the setting squares and setting triangles. Sew into rows as indicated, pressing the seam allowances toward the sashing strips. Stitch the rows together to form the centre of the quilt.

3. Add a $3^1/_2$" x $51^1/_2$" inner border strip to the top and bottom. Find and match the centre points, pinning well before stitching with the blocks uppermost. Press the seams toward the border strip.

Sew the inner borders to each side in the same way. Remove any remaining foundation papers.

4. Add the outer border strips to the quilt. Sew the $6^1/_2$" x $57^1/_2$" borders to the top and bottom first and then the $6^1/_2$" x $94^3/_4$" borders to each side. Find and match the centre points before pinning well and stitching. Press the seams toward the out border.

5. Mark the quilt top with designs of your choice. All seams in Roll'em, Roll'em, Roll'em were quilted in-the-ditch before being quilted as shown.

6. Layer the quilt with the wadding and backing. Pin or baste and then quilt as desired. Bind the edges and add a label.

## SCARECROWS & REINDEER

*Quiltmaker:* Barbara Barber, Hampshire, England, 1996
*Quilt size:* 78" x 78"

In 1996, The Quilt Room in Dorking, Surrey celebrated it's 15th Anniversary.
I made Scarecrows & Reindeer for Pam Lintott and Rosemary Miller, co-owners, to mark the occasion.
The name came from two of the fabrics used which were in The Quilt Room's collection at the time.
The Quilt Room was the shop that introduced me to quilt making
and I have been fond of it ever since.

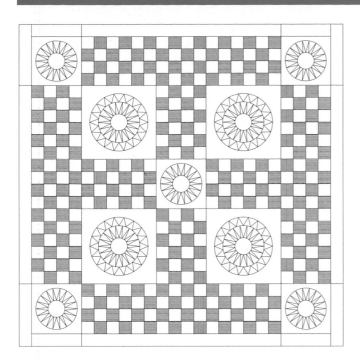

## CUTTING

*From the assorted dark/medium dark prints for the checker-board squares, cut:*
176 squares, each $3^1/_2$" x $3^1/_2$"

*From the assorted light and medium prints for the checker-board squares, cut:*
176 squares, each $3^1/_2$" x $3^1/_2$"

*From the dark red print for the background of the corner squares, cut:*
4 squares, each $12^1/_2$" x $12^1/_2$"

*From the red print for the centre square and the border, cut:*
4 strips, each $3^1/_2$" x $48^1/_2$"
1 square, $12^1/_2$" x $12^1/_2$"

*From the light yellow print for the large blocks and the border corners, cut:*
4 squares, each $18^1/_2$" x $18^1/_2$"
4 strips, each $3^1/_2$" x $15^1/_2$"
4 strips, each $3^1/_2$" x $12^1/_2$"

*For each 12" block, cut:*
2 yellow strips, each $1^1/_4$" x 42". From these strips cut 18 rectangles, each $1^1/_4$" x 4", for the A pieces
1 yellow square, $4^3/_4$" x $4^3/_4$", for the appliquéd centre
1 dark blue strip, 4" x 42". From this strip cut 18 rectangles, each 4" x $2^1/_8$", for the B pieces

*For each 18" block, cut:*
2 red strips, each $1^1/_4$" x 42". From these strips cut 18 rectangles, each $1^1/_4$" x 4", for the A pieces

## MATERIALS:

*44"- wide fabric*

$1^1/_2$ yds. total assorted dark/medium dark red, blue and green prints for checker-board squares

$1^1/_2$ yds. total assorted light and medium yellow, gold and blue prints for checker-board squares

1 yd. dark red print for background of the 4 corner blocks and for binding

$1^3/_8$ yds. red print for background of centre block and the 4 centre sections of border

$1^3/_8$ yds. light yellow print for background of the 4 large blocks and the corner sections of the border

$1^3/_8$ yds. total assorted yellows for blocks

$5/_8$ yd. total assorted dark blues for 12" blocks

$1/_2$ yd. total assorted reds for 18" blocks

$5/_8$ yd. total assorted medium/light blues for 18" blocks

$4^5/_8$ yds. for backing

82" x 82" piece of wadding

26" x 15" piece of freezer paper

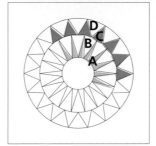

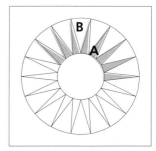

## PHOTOCOPIES

20 copies of Really Sharp Piecing Design*(found on sheets in back pocket of book)*

## CUTTING continued

1 red square, $4^3/_4$" x $4^3/_4$", for the appliquéd centre
1 yellow strip, 4" x 42". From this strip cut 18 rectangles, each 4" x $2^1/_8$", for the B pieces
1 yellow strip, $3^1/_4$" x 42". From this strip cut 18 rectangles, each $3^1/_4$" x $2^1/_8$", for the C pieces
2 medium/light blue strips, each $2^1/_2$" x 42". From these strips cut 18 rectangles, each $2^1/_2$" x $3^1/_4$", for the D pieces

## PIECING

1.  Following the instructions for "2-Ring Circular Piecing" on page 29, make 4 Really Sharp Piecing blocks. Use the $18^1/_2$" x $18^1/_2$" light yellow squares and the 18 rectangles cut for each of the A, B, C and D pieces. Use the red $4^3/_4$" x $4^3/_4$" squares for the appliquéd centres.

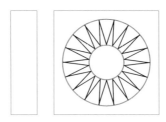
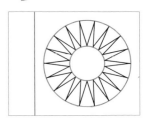

**MAKE 4**

2.  Following the instructions for "1-Ring Circular Piecing" on page 34, make 5 blocks. Use the $12^1/_2$" x $12^1/_2$" squares; 4 from the dark red and 1 from the red print for centre block. Use the 18 rectangles cut for each of the A and B pieces. The yellow $4^3/_4$" x $4^3/_4$" squares are used for appliquéd centres.

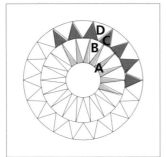

**MAKE 5**

3.  Make the checker-board units using the $3^1/_2$" x $3^1/_2$" squares. Alternate the dark/medium dark squares with the light and medium squares to give a checker-board effect.

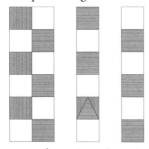

Arrange the squares and sew into the units as shown. For the checker-board units, consistently press the seam allowances toward the dark squares. Press all other seams as indicated by the arrows in the diagrams.

**MAKE 2 OF EACH**

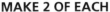
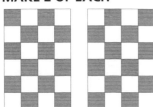

**MAKE 2 OF EACH**

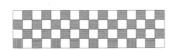

4.  Using 2 of the red print $3^1/_2$" x $48^1/_2$" border strips, sew a $3^1/_2$" x $15^1/_2$" light yellow strip to each end.

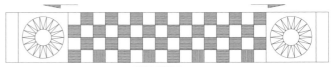

**MAKE 2**

5.  Sew a $3^1/_2$" x $12^1/_2$" light yellow border strip to one side of each of the 4 corner blocks.

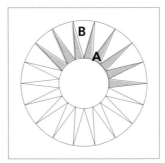

**MAKE 4**

6.  Using an identical set of the long checker-board units and the corner block units, sew together to make 2 long sections.

**MAKE 2**

Add the border units made in step 4.

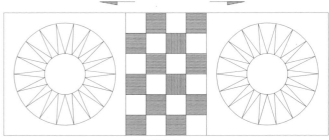

**MAKE 2**

7.  Using an identical set of the smaller checker-board units, sew a large block onto both long sides of the unit.

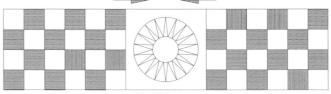

**MAKE 2**

8.  The remaining set of smaller checker-board units is sew to opposite sides of the centre square.

**MAKE 1**

9. Assemble the quilt top according to the diagram.

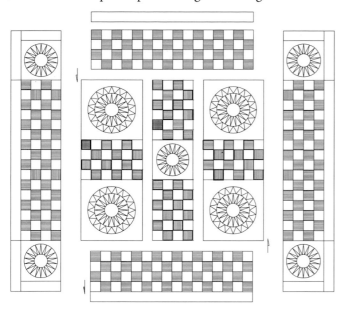

10. Mark the quilting design of your choice on the quilt top. All of the seams in Scarecrows & Reindeer were quilted in-the-ditch. A diagonal grid was then quilted throughout except within the pieced circles.

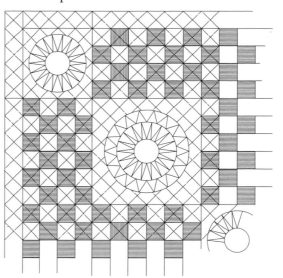

11. Layer the quilt top with the wadding and backing; pin or baste and then quilt as desired. Bind the edges and add a label.

**TEMPLATE**

**COLUMNS
SASHING
BLOCK**

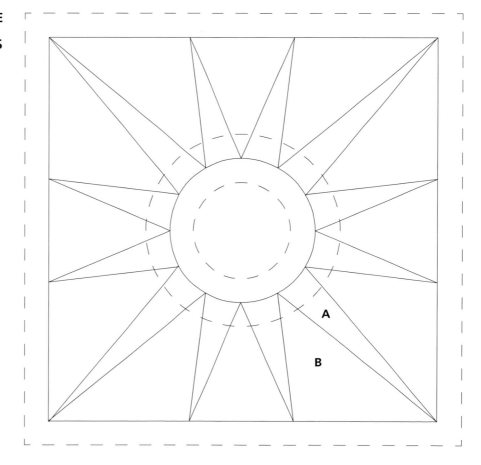

A
B

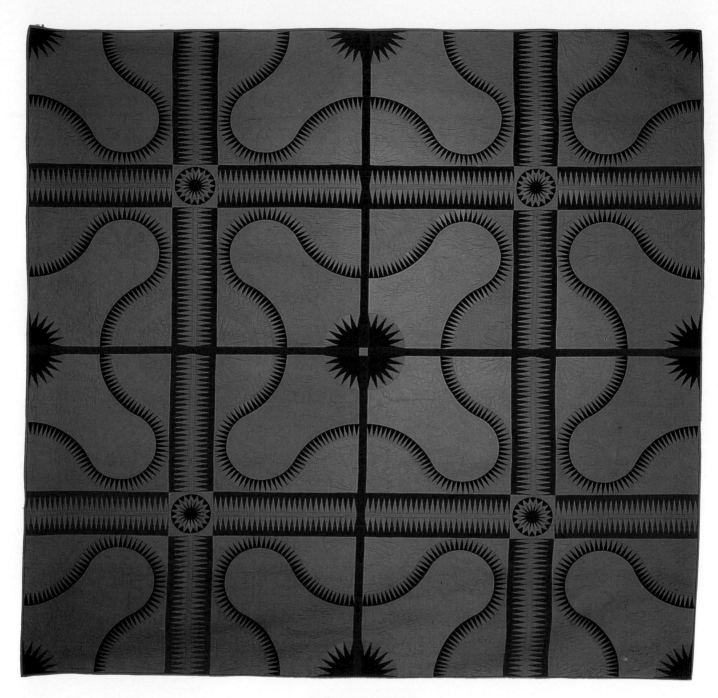

# SOLSTICE

*Quiltmaker:* Barbara Barber, Hampshire, England, 1994
*Quilt size:* 101$\frac{1}{2}$" x 101$\frac{1}{2}$"

Solstice remains a favorite quilt of mine.
Not only has it given me warmth from the many people who have enjoyed it,
but it also gave me the wonderful techniques for Really Sharp Piecing.

## CUTTING

*From the blue, cut;*

2 strips, each 2" x 44". From these strips cut 72 pieces, each 2" x ³/₄", for the A pieces in the 4 small sashing blocks.

4 squares, each 2¹/₂" x 2¹/₂", for the appliquéd centres in the 4 small sashing blocks.

4 strips, each 3¹/₂" x 44". From these strips cut 112 pieces, each 3¹/₂" x 1¹/₄", for the F pieces in the large blocks.

2 strips, each 4¹/₄" x 44". Refer to "Photocopied Templates" on page 26. Using photocopies, cut 16 of the E pieces.

*From the red, cut:*

NOTE: *Cut the 50¹/₂" long strips from the lengthwise grain of the fabric first.*

4 strips, each 2" x 50¹/₂". These strips form the red cross through the centre of the quilt.

32 strips, each 1¹/₄" x 22¹/₈", for the sashing.

28 strips, each 3" x 44". From these strips cut 896 pieces, each 3" x 1¹/₄", for the red triangles in the sashing units.

*From the green, cut:*

3 strips, each 1¹/₄" x 44". From these strips cut 72 pieces, each 1¹/₄" x 1³/₄", for the D pieces in the 4 small sashing blocks.

25 strips, each 3" x 44". From these strips cut 1024 pieces, each 3" x 1", for the J pieces in the blocks.

*From the orange, cut:*

16 strips, each 1¹/₄" x 22¹/₈", for the sashing.

2 strips, each 2" x 44". From these strips cut 72 pieces, each 2" x 1", for the B pieces in the 4 small sashing blocks.

## MATERIALS:

*44"-wide fabric*

⁷/₈ yd. blue

4 yds. red

2³/₈ yds. green

13¹/₂ yds. orange

9¹/₄ yds. for backing

106" x 106" piece of wadding

Freezer paper as required for large templates - approx. 2 yds. x 15" wide

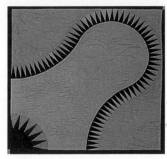

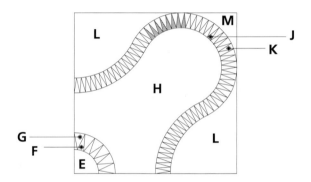

## PHOTOCOPIES

9 copies of Solstice Sashing Block *(page 59)*

32 copies of Solstice Sashing Unit

16 copies of F/G Curved Unit *(found within Solstice Block)*

16 copies of the J/K Curved Unit *(found within Solstice Block)*

Copies as required of E, H, L and M pieces for making templates *(found within Solstice Block)*

1 Copy of Solstice Block to use for the quilting design

*The Solstice Block is a large pattern and printed on the sheets in the back pocket of the book. The quilting design is an important part of the quilt and is included on the block pattern which contains the piecing pattern. During piecing, ignore the quilting design lines on the pattern. Below, on the left, is the piecing pattern with all seam lines and cutting lines. On the right, is the quilting design as it would look without any of the cutting lines. Refer to these as you prepare to cut your photocopies for piecing.*

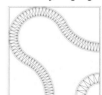

## CUTTING continued

3 strips, each $1^1/_4$" x 44". From these strips cut 72 pieces, each $1^1/_4$" x $1^3/_4$", for the C pieces in the 4 small sashing blocks.

4 squares, each $7^1/_4$" x $7^1/_4$", for the background of the 4 small sashing blocks.

4 strips, each $3^1/_2$" x 44". From these strips cut 96 pieces, each $3^1/_2$" x $1^3/_4$", for the G pieces in the blocks.

32 strips, each 3" x 44". From these strips cut 1040 pieces, each 3" x $1^1/_4$", for the K pieces in the blocks.

27 strips, each 3" x 44". From these strips cut 864 pieces, each 3" x $1^1/_4$", for the orange triangles in the sashing units. 16 pieces cut for each of the pieces H, L, L reversed and M. Refer to "Photocopied Templates" on page 26. Use the freezer paper method to make templates for these large pieces. Remember to mark placement points on all of the curved fabric edges in order to match them up with the foundation units when sewing them together.

1 square, 2" x 2", for the square in the very centre of the quilt.

## PIECING

1. Using the $7^1/_4$" x $7^1/_4$" orange background squares, the $2^1/_2$" x $2^1/_2$" blue squares for the appliquéd centres and the pieces cut for the A, B, C and D pieces, make 4 Solstice Sashing Blocks. Refer to "2-Ring Piecing" on page 29. Although this is a small block, it can be sewn together in the usual way, using your sewing machine. However, for ease, you may wish to consider hand appliqué as an alternative when joining the inner ring unit to the outer ring unit. This should be done after sewing the outer ring into the background square by machine and after you have appliquéd the centre onto the inner ring.

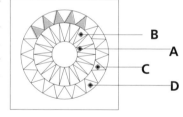

2. Using the photocopies of Solstice Sashing Unit, make 32 units. Refer to "Straight Unit Piecing" on page 36. Alternate red and orange pieces, starting and ending with a red piece. Trim all of these sashing units as described in "Trimming" on page 36.

**MAKE 32**

Sew a $1^1/_4$" x $22^1/_8$" red sashing strip to each of these sashing units. Be sure to attach the red strip to the side of the unit which is edged with red triangles. Find and match the centres and pin together well. Stitch with the paper foundation on top, using the line as a stitching guide to keep the points really sharp. Press the seam towards the red strip. Sew a $1^1/_4$" x $22^1/_8$" orange sashing strip to the other side of half of the sashing units. Press the seam towards the orange strip. Sew the remaining sashing units onto the free edge of the orange strip, pressing the seam towards the orange.

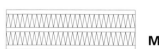

**MAKE 16**

Remove all of the paper foundations from the sashing units except for the last 2 or 3 triangles at each end of the foundations. The paper triangles that are left intact will be helpful in keeping those points sharp when sewing the sashing units together with the sashing squares.

3. The large blocks are pieced using the "Curved Unit" method on page 34. In this block there are two curved units, a large one and a small one. Although there are two curved units within the block you still put the block together in the same way as a block with a single curved unit. As you add pieces to the curved units be sure to match points along the curves and pin well. For all the curved seams throughout the block, press the seam allowances away from the foundation curved unit.

Piece the F/G Units using the blue and orange pieces. Alternate blue and orange pieces, starting and ending with a blue piece. Add the E piece to this unit.

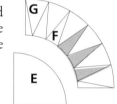

Sew this unit onto the H piece.

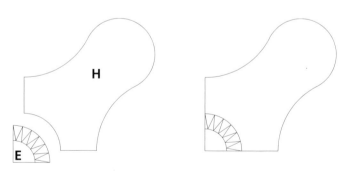

Piece the J/K Units using the orange and green pieces. Alternate orange and green pieces, starting and ending with an orange piece.

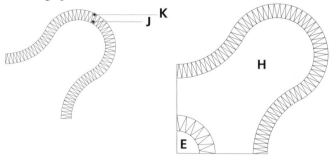

Sew this J/K Unit onto the H Unit.

Add an L piece to one side and the L piece reversed to the other side of the unit.

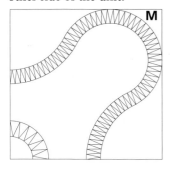 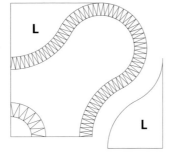

**MAKE 16 BLOCKS**                    **REVERSED**

Stitch on the M piece to complete the block.

4.  Sew one block to each side of 8 of the sashing units. Find and match the centres and pin carefully. Stitch with the block uppermost, using the foundation line as a guide in the area where the curved unit touches the sashing. Press the seam towards the sashing unit.

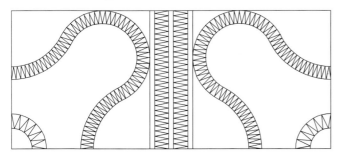

5.  Stitch a sashing unit to both sides of the four sashing blocks. Stitch with the sashing unit uppermost and press the seam towards the sashing.

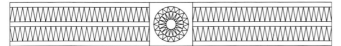

6.  Sew one of the units made in Step 4 to each side of the units made in Step 5. Press the seam towards the sashing.

7.  Lay out the prepared units with the red strips and the orange centre square. Stitch together as shown. Remove any remaining foundation papers from the quilt.

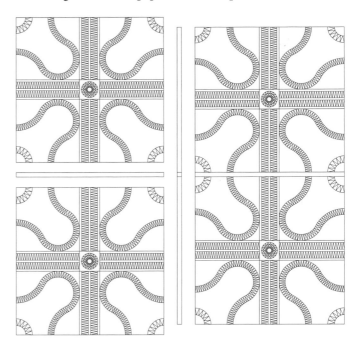

8. Mark the top using the quilting design printed on the Solstice Block pattern. This can be done easily with a light box. If the fabric is very light coloured, you may be able to simply trace the design through the fabric without the aid of a light box. This will be made easier if you darken the lines on the copy of the quilting design with a permanent black felt tip marker. All seams of Solstice were quilted in-the-ditch before the designs were quilted and then the background was stipple quilted.

9.  Layer the quilt top with the wadding and backing. Pin or baste and then quilt as desired. Bind the quilt with orange fabric and add a label.

## SPRING GREENS

*Quiltmaker:* Barbara Barber, Hampshire, England, 1996
*Quilt size:* 85$^1$/$_2$" x 85$^1$/$_2$"

Green was definitely the "in" colour for clothing from the spring of 1996.
Although my wardrobe may not have reflected this,
I will have a more enduring record of this fashion event with Spring Greens.
My thanks go to Myra Ibbetson who, when time ran short, gave me much appreciated help
with the piecing and quilting.

# SPRING GREENS

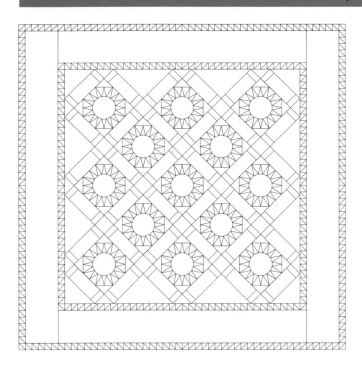

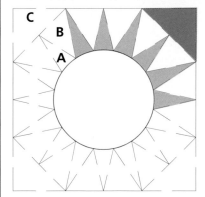

## MATERIALS:

*44"-wide fabric*

2 yds. total assorted beige prints for blocks

2 yds. total assorted blue and purple prints for blocks

$2^5/8$ yds. green print for blocks, setting triangles and pieced borders

$2^1/4$ yds. black print for pieced borders, sashing squares, sashing triangles and binding

$^1/2$ yd. light print for sashing

$3^3/8$ yds. blue/green print for sashing and borders

$5^1/4$ yds. for backing

90" x 90" piece of wadding

## CUTTING

*For each block, cut:*

2 beige strips, each $2^3/4$" x 44". From these strips cut 16 rectangles, each $2^3/4$" x 4" for the B pieces

1 blue or purple strip, $3^3/4$" x 44". From this strip cut 16 rectangles, each $3^3/4$" x $1^3/4$" for the A pieces

1 blue or purple square, $7^1/2$" x $7^1/2$" for the appliquéd centre

*From the green print, cut:*

4 strips, each $4^3/4$" x 44". From these strips cut 26 squares, each $4^3/4$" x $4^3/4$". Cut each square once diagonally for 52 C pieces in the blocks.

15 strips, each $3^1/4$" x 44". From these strips cut 172 squares, each $3^1/4$" x $3^1/4$". Cut each square once diagonally for 344 triangles for the pieced borders.

2 squares, each $16^7/8$" x $16^7/8$". Cut each square twice diagonally for the 8 side setting triangles.

2 squares, each $8^5/8$" x $8^5/8$". Cut each square once diagonally for the 4 corner triangles.

## PHOTOCOPIES

26 copies of Spring Greens Block *(found on sheets in back pocket of book)*

Copies as required to make border foundations using Spring Greens Border Sections 1 and 2 *(found on sheets in back pocket of book)*

## CUTTING continued

*From the black print, cut:*

15 strips, each 3¹/₄" x 44". From these strips cut 172 squares, each 3¹/₄" x 3¹/₄". Cut each square once diagonally for 344 triangles for the pieced borders.

2 strips, each 4" x 44". From this strip cut 12 squares, each 4" x 4" for the sashing squares.

3 squares, each 6¹/₄" x 6¹/₄". Cut each square twice diagonally for the 12 sashing triangles.

*From the light print, cut:*

4 strips, each 4" x 44". From these strips cut 72 rectangles, each 4" x 2", for the sashing.

*From the blue/green print, cut:*

4 strips, each 8¹/₂" x 44". From theses strips cut 36 rectangles, each 8¹/₂" x 4", for the sashing.

2 strips, each 65¹/₂" x 9", for the borders.

2 strips, each 82¹/₂" x 9", for the borders.

## PIECING

1. Following the instructions for "Non-Circular Blocks" on page 35, make 13 Spring Green blocks. When cutting the photocopy, cut the block as a square, leaving the corner triangles intact. The corners are sewn with foundation piecing onto the completed ring as detailed in "Non-Circular Blocks". Use 16 rectangles cut for each of the A and B pieces and 4 of the green C pieces for each block. A 7¹/₂" x 7¹/₂" blue or purple square is used for the appliquéd centre.

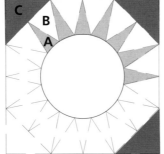

Trim the outer edges of the blocks, referring to "Trimming" on page 36.

**MAKE 13**

2. Stitch 2" x 4" light print rectangles to both ends of all of the 4" x 8¹/₂" blue/green print sashing strips. Press seams to one side.

3. Refer to the diagram as needed to lay out the blocks, sashing strips, sashing squares, sashing triangles, setting triangles and corner triangles. Join the units in each diagonal row. When sewing the blocks together, stitch on the paper foundation sewing on the line. Press the seam allowances towards the sashing strips. Join the rows, matching the seams. Press seam allowances towards the sashing. Remove the paper foundations from the pieced blocks.

4. Prepare the paper foundations for the inner pieced border by gluing together copies of the Spring Greens Border Sections. To ensure accuracy, overlap the units by one whole square when gluing the copies together. For more information about gluing photocopied designs together see page 23. When preparing foundation papers for a long string of piecing, I find it very helpful to number the individual units. By writing numbers on the foundations, I am certain to end up with the correct size border strip which has the correct number of pieces. Glue the photocopies together to make foundation units as shown. When planning your colour arrangement, remember that paper piecing produces a mirror image effect. When piecing something like this border where the colour sequence changes within the unit, I may write the colour of the piece on the foundations to help keep it clear in my mind.

**MAKE 2 OF EACH**

Piece the inner border sections using the green print and the black print triangles, referring to "Straight Unit Piecing" on page 36. Trim the units, referring to "Trimming" on page 36.

5. Add the pieced borders to the central section of the quilt. Find and match up centre points before pinning well and stitching on the line of the paper foundation. Press seam allowances away from the pieced borders. *See next page.*

6. Stitch a blue/green print 9" x 65¹/₂" strip to top and

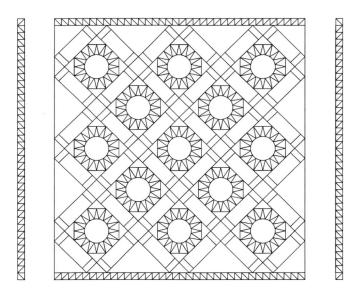

bottom of quilt. Add a 9" x 82$^1/_2$" strip to each side. Remember to find and match up centre points. Pin well before stitching on the line of the paper foundation. Press seam allowances away from the inner pieced border. Remove paper foundations from the inner pieced border.

7. Prepare the paper foundations for the outer pieced borders by gluing together copies of the Spring Greens Border Sections. Form the paper foundation units shown, referring to Step 4.

**MAKE 2 OF EACH**

Piece the outer border sections using the green print and the black print triangles, referring to "Straight Unit Piecing" on page 36. Trim the units, referring to "Trimming" on page 36.

8. Sew the outer borders onto the quilt in the same way as the inner pieced borders were sewn.

Press the seams away from the pieced border.

12. Mark the quilt top with designs of your choice. All seams in Spring Greens were quilted in-the-ditch before quilting as shown.

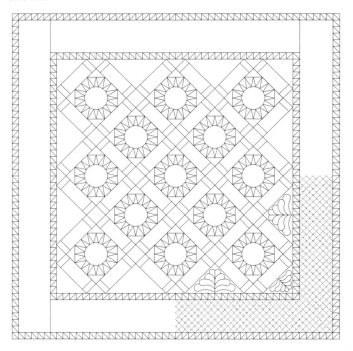

13. Just before layering the top, wadding and backing, carefully remove the paper foundations from the pieced border. Leaving the papers intact on the outer edges until just before layering the quilt will prevent the pieced section from stretching out of shape. Layer the top, wadding and backing. Pin or baste and then quilt as desired. Bind the edges and add a label.

# SUNFLOWERS

*Quiltmaker:* Cathy Corbishley Michel, London, England, 1997
*Quilt size:* 43¹/₂" x 43¹/₂"

Cathy says that when she first saw the design, sunflowers sprang to mind.
Her choice of colours certainly enhances that idea.
This cheery quilt would be great as either a cot quilt or a wall hanging.

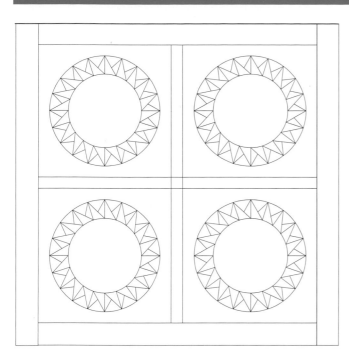

## CUTTING

*From the black print, cut:*
4 squares, each $18^1/_2$" x $18^1/_2$", for the background of the blocks.

*From the red print, cut:*
4 strips, each 2" x $18^1/_2$", for the sashing.
2 strips, each $3^1/_2$" x 38", for the top and bottom borders.
2 strips, each $3^1/_2$" x 44", for the side borders.

*From the gold print, cut:*
4 strips, each 4" x 44". From these strips cut 80 pieces, each 4" x $1^3/_4$", for the A pieces.

*From the yellow print, cut:*
3 strips, each $3^1/_4$" x 44". From these strips cut 80 pieces, each $3^1/_4$" x $1^1/_2$", for the B pieces.

*From the green print, cut:*
5 strips, each 3" x 44". From these strips cut 80 pieces, each 3" x $2^1/_2$", for the C pieces.
Binding strips were cut 3" wide for this extra wide double fold binding.

*From the novelty sunflower print, cut:*
1 square, 2" x 2".

*From the orange print, cut:*
4 squares, each 11" x 11", for the appliquéd centres.

## MATERIALS:

*44"- wide fabric*

$1^1/_8$ yds. black print for the blocks

$1^3/_8$ yds. red print for the sashing and the border

$1/_2$ yd. gold print for the A pieces

$3/_8$ yd. yellow print for the B pieces

$7/_8$ yd. green print for the C pieces and the binding

2" x 2" square novelty sunflower print for the centre square

$5/_8$ yd. orange print for the appliquéd centres

$2^5/_8$ yds. for the backing

48" x 48" piece of wadding

15" x 15" piece of freezer paper

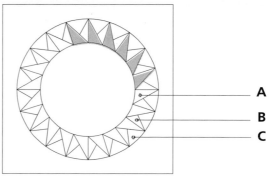

## PHOTOCOPIES

9 copies of Sunflowers Design *(found on sheets in back pocket of book)*

## PIECING

1. Following the instructions for "1-Ring Circular Piecing" on page 34, make 4 blocks. Use the 18½" x 18½" squares, and the pieces cut for the A, B and C pieces. The 11" x 11" squares are for the appliquéd centres. Most Ring Piecing can be done by adding pieces around the circle, starting in either direction. In this block, however, it can only be pieced in one direction. Make the cut through the ring in the position indicated and start piecing in the direction of the arrow. The numbers show the order in which the pieces are added. Carry on around the circle in this way.

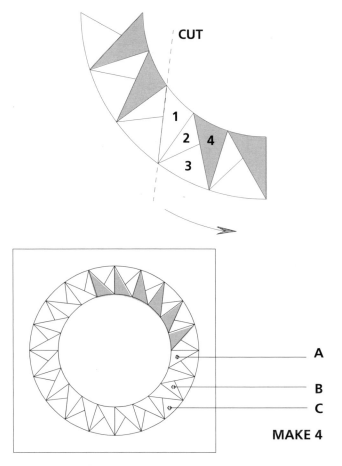

MAKE 4

2. Lay the blocks out with the sashing strips and the centre square. Join these to form rows, pressing the seam allowances toward the sashing strips. Sew the rows together to form the centre of the quilt. Add the 3½" x 38" border strips to the top and bottom. Find and match the centres before pinning and stitching. Press seams to one side.

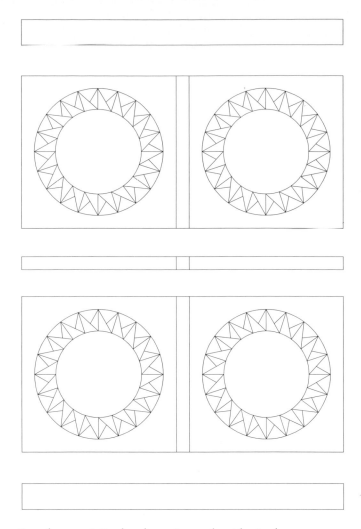

Sew the remaining border strips to the sides in the same way.

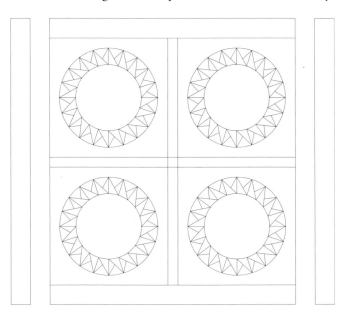

3. Mark the quilting designs of your choice on the quilt top. All of the seams in Sunflowers were quilted in-the-ditch before being quilted as shown.

4. Layer the quilt top with the wadding and backing; pin or baste and then quilt as desired. Bind the edges and add a label.

**TEMPLATE**

**ROLL'EM SASHING BLOCK**

D

C

B

A

## SUNNY SIDE UP

*Quiltmaker:* Maggie Barber, London, England, 1997
*Quilt size:* 72$\frac{1}{2}$" x 72$\frac{1}{2}$"

Scrap quilts have always been perennial favorites with quiltmakers as well as collectors.
This one is a glorious quilt with a stunning array of fabrics.
It certainly leaves me feeling "Sunny Side Up"!

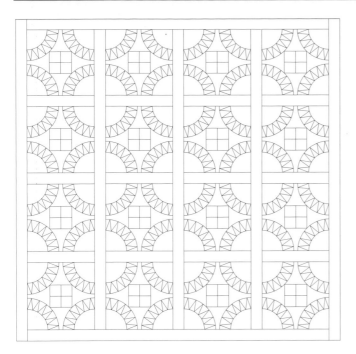

## CUTTING

*From the assorted dark prints, cut:*
16 strips, each $3^1/2$" x 44". From these strips cut 384 rectangles, each $3^1/2$" x $1^3/4$" for the A pieces.

*From the assorted medium prints, cut:*
25 strips, each $3^1/2$" x 44". From these strips cut 448 rectangles, each $3^1/2$" x $2^1/4$" for the B pieces.

*From the remainder of the assorted dark and medium prints, cut:*
5 strips, each 3" x 44". From these strips cut 64, each 3" x 3" for the E pieces.
Segments cut to lengths varying between 3" and 5" long and 2" wide for a double fold binding. Cut enough pieces to sew together in a long strip to make the full length of the binding.

*From the off-white, cut:*
8 strips, each $5^1/2$" x 44". Refer to "Photocopied Templates" on page 26. Using photocopies, cut 64 of the C pieces.

*From the dark blue print, cut:*
6 strips, each 7" x 44". Refer to "Photocopied Templates" on page 26. Using photocopies, cut 64 of the D pieces.

*From the dark red print for the sashing, cut:*
*NOTE: Cut the long strips from the lengthwise grain of the fabric first.*
2 strips, each 3" x 73"
5 strips, each 3" x $67^1/2$"
12 strips, each 3" x $15^1/2$"

## MATERIALS:

*44"-wide fabric*

$2^1/8$ yds. total assorted dark prints for the A and E pieces and the binding.

3 yds. total assorted medium prints for the B and E pieces and the binding.

$1^1/4$ yds. off-white for the C pieces

$1^1/4$ yds. dark blue print for the D pieces

$2^1/4$ yds. dark red print for the sashing

$4^1/4$ yds. for backing

77" x 77" piece of wadding

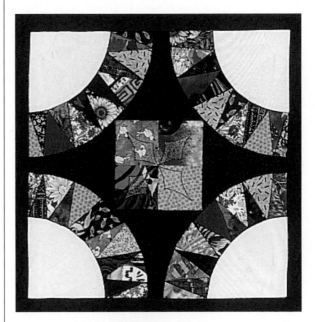

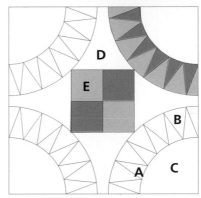

## PHOTOCOPIES

64 copies of Sunny Curved Unit *(page 99)*

Copies of the Sunny D piece as needed *(found on sheets in back pocket of book)*

## PIECING

1. To make the centre section of the blocks, sew all of the 3" x 3" squares into pairs of dark and medium. Join the pairs to make a 4-patch unit. Press seam to one side.

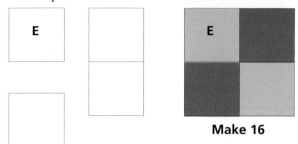

**Make 16**

2. Fold a D piece in half and pinch this fold on the longer straight side to indicate the centre. Match this crease with the centre seam of the 4-patch unit. Pin and sew with right sides together. Press the seam towards the D piece. Repeat on the opposite side. Complete remaining sides in the same way.

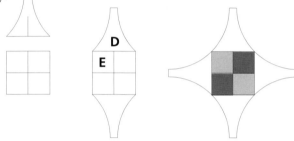

3. This unit will now be the "background" for the 4 curved units in the block. Complete the block using the assorted prints cut for the A and B pieces and the off-white C pieces. Refer to "Curved Units" on page 34. Make 16 blocks.

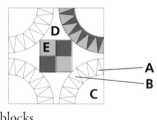

4. Arrange the blocks with the sashing strips. Sew the short sashing strips to the blocks to form rows. Join the rows together with the sashing strips which were cut 3" x 67¹/₂". Press seam allowances toward the sashing.

5. Sew the outer sashing strips onto the quilt.

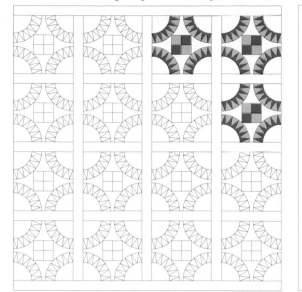

Press the seams toward the sashing. Remove the remaining paper foundations.

6. Mark the top with the quilting design of your choice. All seams of Sunny Side Up were quilted in-the-ditch before being quilted as shown.

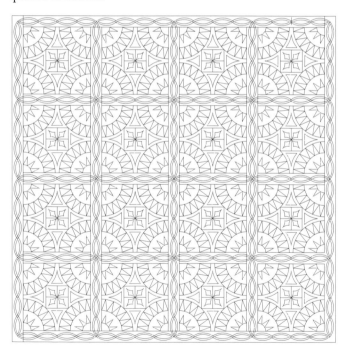

7. Layer the top, wadding and backing. Pin or baste and then quilt.

8. Sew together the segments which were cut 2" wide for the binding. When stitching these segments together, use a stitch length of about 15 stitches per inch. This is a slightly shorter stitch length than is used for normal seams. Press the seams open. Keep stitching these together until the strip is long enough to bind the quilt. Use it to bind the edges and then add a label to complete.

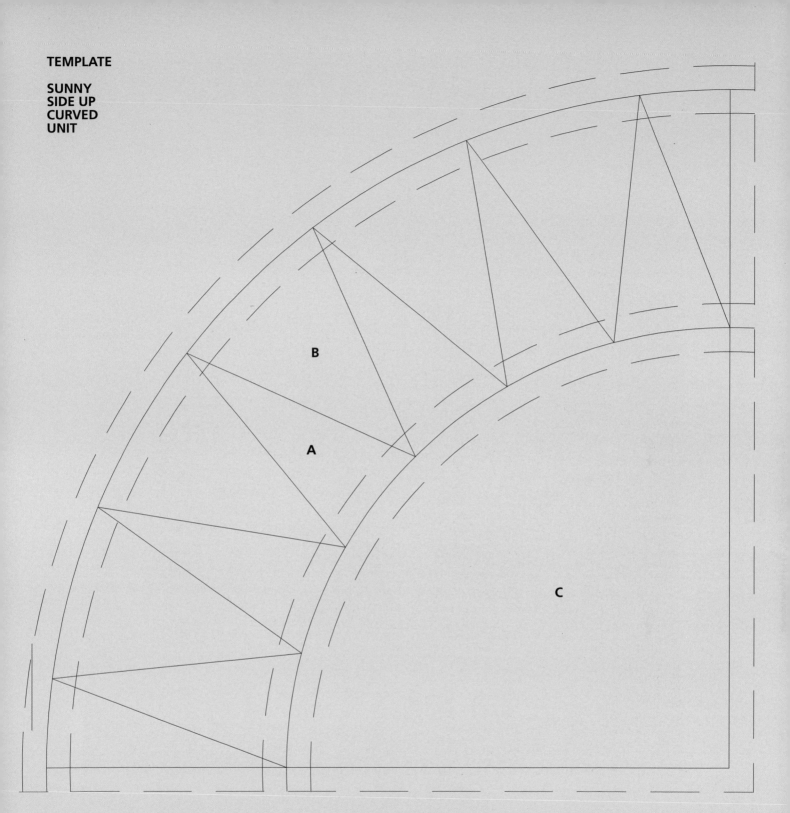

## SWEET WRAPPER

*Quiltmaker:* Phoebe Bartleet, Hampshire, England, 1996
*Quilt size:* 36" x 44"

It's not surprising that this cot quilt ended up with a rather sentimental name
because during the making of it Phoebe became a first-time grandmother.
When you look at this quilt, you can't help feeling that Phoebe hopes her granddaughter
will enjoy colour as much as she herself does.

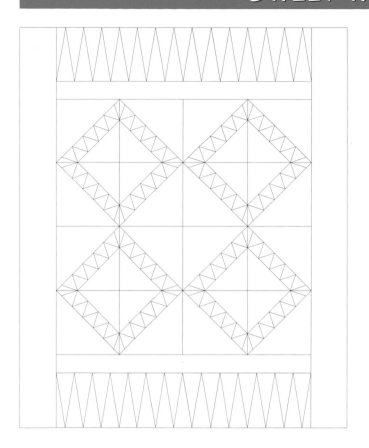

## MATERIALS:

*44"-wide fabric*

$1^1/_4$ yds. turquoise polka dot

$^3/_4$ yd. light green

$^1/_2$ yd. small blue print

$^3/_8$ yd. green polka dot

$^3/_4$ yd. large blue print

$1^3/_8$ yds. for backing

40" x 48" piece of wadding

## CUTTING

*From the turquoise polka dot, cut:*

*NOTE: Cut the long borders from the lengthwise grain of the fabric first.*

2 strips, each $4^1/_2$" x $44^1/_2$", for the side borders.

15 rectangles, each $3^3/_4$" x 7". Cut each rectangle once diagonally for 30 triangles in the top and bottom borders.

4 squares, each $5^1/_2$" x $5^1/_2$". Cut each square once diagonally for the C pieces in 8 of the blocks.

*From the light green, cut:*

4 strips, each $2^3/_4$" x 44". From these strips cut 80 pieces, each $2^3/_4$" x 2", for the A pieces

3 strips, each $3^3/_4$" x 44". From these strips cut 14 rectangles, each $3^3/_4$" x 7". Cut each rectangle once diagonally for 28 triangles in the top and bottom borders.

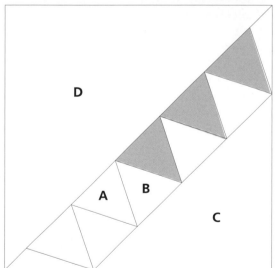

## PHOTOCOPIES

16 copies Sweet Wrapper Unit *(page 63)*

Copies as required of Sweet Wrapper Border *(found on sheets in back pocket of book)*

*From the small blue print, cut:*
5 strips, each 2³/₄" x 44". From these strips cut 96 pieces, each 2³/₄" x 2", for the B pieces.

*From the green polka dot, cut:*
2 strips, each 2¹/₂" x 28¹/₂", for the top and bottom borders.
2 squares, each 5¹/₂" x 5¹/₂". Cut each square once diagonally for the C pieces in 4 of the blocks.

2 squares, each 7⁷/₈" x 7⁷/₈". Cut each square once diagonally for the D pieces in 4 of the blocks.

*From the large blue print, cut:*
6 squares, each 7⁷/₈" x 7⁷/₈". Cut each square once diagonally for the D pieces in 12 of the blocks.

2 squares, each 5¹/₂" x 5¹/₂". Cut each square once diagonally for the C pieces in 4 of the blocks.

## PIECING

*NOTE:* This quilt is made up of 16 blocks. The blocks are all pieced from the same pattern. The effect is achieved by altering the colours within the blocks. This quilt requires 3 different colour arrangements in the blocks. To make the quilt as shown, use the following colour arrangements for the blocks:

4 blocks using the large blue print for both the C and the D pieces
8 blocks using the large blue print for the D pieces and the turquoise polka dot for the C pieces
4 blocks using the green polka dot for both the C and the D pieces

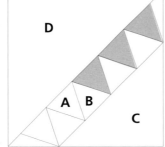

1. Referring to "Straight Unit Piecing" on page 36, piece 16 Sweet Wrapper Units. Use the light green pieces and the small blue print pieces cut for the A and B pieces. Trim all the units as described in "Trimming" on page 36.

**MAKE 16**

2. Fold a C piece in half and pinch the fold on the long edge to mark the centre. Position this crease, right sides together, of the centre mark of the shorter side of a pieced unit. Pin the C piece in place and stitch with the paper on top. Press the seam away from the pieced unit.

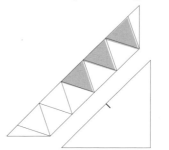 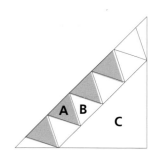

Sew the D piece to the other side of the pieced unit in the same way.

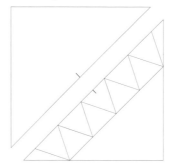 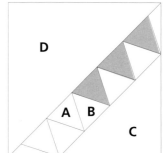

3. Lay the blocks out in the correct colour arrangement, referring to the photograph. Sew the blocks together to form rows, pressing the seam allowances as indicated by the arrows. Join the rows, pressing seams to one side, to form the centre of the quilt.

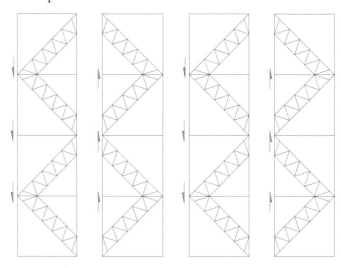

4. Add a 2¹/₂" x 28¹/₂" green polka dot strip to the top and the bottom edges. Find and match the centres before pinning and then stitching with the blocks uppermost. Press the seams away from the blocks.

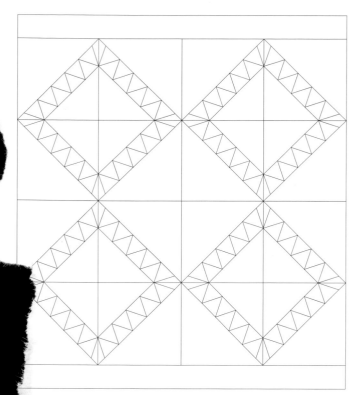

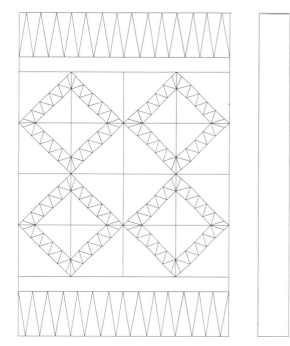

5. Prepare the paper foundations for the pieced border by gluing together copies of Sweet Wrapper Border. To ensure accuracy, overlap the units by one whole triangle when gluing the copies together. For more information about gluing photocopied designs together, see page 23. When preparing foundation papers for a long string of piecing, I find it very helpful to number the individual units. By writing directly on the foundations, I am certain to end up with the correct size strip which has the correct number of pieces. Glue the photocopies together to make foundation units as shown.

**MAKE 2 BORDER FOUNDATIONS**

6. Piece the borders, using the turquoise polka dot and the light green triangles, referring to "Straight Unit Piecing" on page 36. Trim the borders as described in "Trimming" on page 36.

7. Add the pieced borders to the top and the bottom of the quilt. Find and match up the centres before pinning well and stitching on the line of the paper foundation. Press seam allowances away from the pieced borders.

Add $4^1/_2$" x $44^1/_2$" turquoise polka dot border to each side of the quilt. Find and match the centres and pin before stitching with the blocks uppermost. Press seams toward the borders.

8. Remove the remaining paper foundations from the blocks. Mark the top with quilting designs of your choice. All seams of Sweet Wrapper were quilted in-the-ditch before quilting as shown in the picture on page 100.

9. Just before layering the top, wadding and backing, carefully remove the paper foundations from the pieced borders. Leaving the papers intact on the outer edges until just before layering the quilt will prevent the pieced section from stretching out of shape. Layer the top, wadding and backing. Pin or baste and then quilt as desired. Bind the edges and add a label.

## QUILTING VIDEOS by Barbara Barber

### "COMPLETELY QUILTED"
*running time 105 minutes.*

This video is a complete guide to machine quilting. It covers all the necessary steps as well as hints and tips for achieving beautiful quilting with your sewing machine.

### "REALLY SHARP PIECING"
*running time 115 minutes.*

Covering the techniques in this book, the video shows each step in a clearly presented workshop format. Seeing it done makes it easy.

Both videos have been professionally produced with excellent close-ups and are available from:

**PB Publications**
Ramridge Dene
Weyhill, Andover
Hants
SP11 0QP
*Tel: 01264 772465*

## QUILT SHOPS AND SUPPLIERS

These are just a very few of the many excellent U.K. suppliers:

**The Contented Cat**
Flint Cottage
Treacle Lane
Rushden, Buntingford
Herts. SG9 0SL
*Tel: 01763 288234*

**The Cotton Patch**
1285 Stratford Road
Hall Green
Birmingham B28 9AJ
*Tel: 0121 702 2840*

**Country Threads**
2 Pierrepoint Place
Bath BA1 1JX
*Tel: 01225 480056*

**Green Hill**
27 Bell Street
Romsey
Hants. SO51 8GY
*Tel: 01794 517973*

**Piecemakers**
15 Manor Green Road
Epsom
Surrey KT19 8RA
*Tel: 01372 743161*

**Quilt Basics**
Unit 19 Chiltern House
Waterside, Chesham
Bucks. HP5 1PS
*Tel: 01494 791401*

**Quilters Haven**
68 High Street
Wickham Market
Suffolk
*Tel: 01728 746275*

**The Quilt Room**
20 West Street
Dorking
Surrey RH4 1BL
*Tel: 01306 740739*

**Moor Silks & Yarns**
Paddons Row, Brook Street
Tavistock
Devon PL19 0HF
*Tel: 01822 612624*